WH

RU

WHO'S WHO
IN
RUGBY LEAGUE

Queen Anne Press

WHO'S WHO IN SPORT SERIES
Edited by David Emery
Published by Queen Anne Press

1984 titles
WHO'S WHO IN FLAT RACING
WHO'S WHO IN INTERNATIONAL CRICKET
WHO'S WHO IN INTERNATIONAL RUGBY

A QUEEN ANNE PRESS BOOK
© Copyright First Editions (Rambletree Limited) 1984
First published in 1984 by
Queen Anne Press, a division of
Macdonald & Co (Publishers) Ltd
London and Sydney

A BPCC plc Company

*Cover photograph Brian Lockwood
by Tony Duffy/Allsport*

ISBN 0 356 10435 4 (cased)
      0 356 10436 2 (paper)

Typeset by Vigo Press Limited
Printed and bound in Great Britain by
The Pitman Press, Bath
Designed, edited and produced by First Editions,
Chancery House, 319 City Road, London EC1V 1LJ

Macdonald & Co (Publishers) Ltd
Maxwell House
74 Worship Street
London EC2A 2EN

Introduction

Rugby League began as a form of professional Rugby Union on August 29, 1894. Twenty clubs from Yorkshire and Lancashire agreed to resign their membership of the Union code after a long-running row about broken time payments. The Northern clubs believed players should be compensated for working hours lost; their Southern counterparts did not agree.

Since those beginnings, the 13-a-side game has swept from the North of England across to Europe and Australasia. It has also gained a foothold in the South of England, with clubs such as Fulham, and in South Wales, at Cardiff.

The annual pilgrimage to Wembley for the Challenge Cup Final has become a highlight of the sporting calendar, both for the calibre of competition and for the trouble-free deportment of the supporters.

Who's Who in Rugby League looks at the established players across the world and also pinpoints the young stars of the future.

The game remains, essentially, a part-time sport and so player movement between clubs is extensive. Information in this book was correct on June 1, 1984.

Mick Adams

Born: September 28, 1951, Widnes, Cheshire, England.
Height: 5ft 11in.   *Weight:* 13st 7lb.
Position: Loose Forward.
Club: Widnes.
Great Britain Honours
Debut (full): June 1979 v Australia (in Sydney)
Appearances (full): five (one as sub).
Club Honours
Division one: winners 1977/78
Challenge Cup: winners 1974/75, 1978/79, 1980/81, 1983/84; runners up 1975/76, 1976/77, 1981/82
Premiership Trophy: winners 1979/80, 1981/82, 1982/83; runners up 1977/78
John Player Trophy: winners 1975/76, 1978/79; runners up 1974/75, 1977/78, 1979/80, 1983/84
Lancashire Cup: winners 1974/75, 1975/76, 1976/77, 1978/79, 1979/80; runners up 1981/82, 1983/84
BBC Floodlit Final: winners 1978/79
Awards: Trumanns Man of Steel Division One Player of the Year-1979 and 1980
Man of the Match Award: Lancashire Cup Final 1979/80.

One of the most popular players to have worn Widnes's white jersey, Mick Adams has been with the club since 1970 and was honoured with club captaincy in the 1980/81 season. Of all his outstanding matches, his performance in the 1979/80 Lancashire Cup final must rank near the top. Scorer of one try, he played a magnificent game to be Man of the Match as Widnes beat Workington 11-0. He was first capped by England in the 1975 World Championships, making his debut in the game with New Zealand at Bradford. His current team-mate Stuart Wright also made his debut that day.

Mick toured Australasia with Great Britain in 1979, making his debut in the second Test in Sydney and marrying his Australian wife, Christine, during the tour. He had two summer spells in New Zealand with Canterbury Bankstown and toured Down Under again in 1984. He was honoured with the Trumanns Man of Steel Division One Player of the Year award in both 1979 and 1980.

His loyalty to Widnes was rewarded with a benefit in 1982. Mick represented Widnes at swimming and athletics as a schoolboy and still has a keen interest in both sports.

Jack Addy

Born: Dewsbury, West Yorkshire, England.
Height: 5ft 8in.   *Weight:* 13st 0lb.
Position: Coach.
Club: Dewsbury.

Jack played for his home town team of Dewsbury and spent his spare time coaching amateurs in the area. At Crown Flatt he appeared alongside current Leeds coach Maurice Bamford and when Maurice Bamford took the Halifax coaching job he asked Jack to join as assistant. They went on to work together at Huddersfield, Wigan and Bramley before Maurice moved to Leeds in 1983. Jack returned to Dewsbury to take up his first senior coaching job in his own right.

Allan Agar

Born: October 8, 1948,

Featherstone, West Yorkshire, England.
Height: 5ft 9in.   *Weight:* 13st 0lb.
Position: Coach, Featherstone Rovers.
Club: Featherstone Rovers.
Club Honours
Division One: winners 1978/79 (Hull KR)
Challenge Cup: winners 1979/80 (Hull KR) winners 1982/83 (Featherstone – coach)
Yorkshire Cup: runners up 1972/73 (Dewsbury)
Championship Play-off: winners 1972/73 (Dewsbury)
BBC Floodlit Trophy: runners up 1979/80 (Hull KR)
Awards: Trumanns Man of Steel 1983.

Featherstone Rovers' shock Challenge Cup final victory over Hull in 1983 was a personal triumph for coach Allan Agar. He had almost resigned shortly before the start of Rovers' cup run because his wife was seriously ill. But he persevered and was rewarded not only with that cup win but with his wife's recovery as well.

Featherstone bred, he joined his home town club the day after his 17th birthday in 1965. He did not quite make it first time around and moved to Dewsbury in 1969. Three years later Dewsbury landed a huge upset when, finishing eighth in the League Championship, they proceded to win the Championship Play-off. Allan scored one of their tries in the final against Leeds. Allan, a scrum half or stand off, moved to New Hunslet in 1975, but after two barren seasons he joined Hull Kingston Rovers. Success followed: a First Division Championship winners medal in 1978/79, and,

the following season, a Challenge Cup triumph with a 10-5 victory over Hull.

Allan moved to Wakefield in a £4,000 deal for the start of the next season, but after less than a year he was appointed player/coach of the newly formed Carlisle team. That first season at Carlisle, 1981/82, Allan scored 12 tries, including the 100th of his career in the match with Keighley. After guiding Carlisle to the First Division, Allan resigned and eventually took over the reins at Featherstone, where it had all started 17 years earlier. Just five months later he was leading the team out at Wembley.

Fred Ah Kuoi

Born: June 7, 1956, Auckland, New Zealand.
Height: 5ft 11in   *Weight:* 12st 5lb.
Position: Stand off.
Club: Hull.
New Zealand Honours
Debut (full): 1975 v Australia
Appearances (full): 20.
Club Honours
Division One: runners up 1983/84
New Zealand Player of the Year: 1979.

An exciting addition to the Hull side, Fred Ah Kuoi came to the Boulevard in February 1984 as a replacement for Peter Sterling who returned to Australia. And Fred soon settled into the back line which contained fellow Kiwis Leuluai, O'Hara and Kemble. He gained his first New Zealand cap in 1975 and is the most experienced of the current New Zealand Test players – along with team mate Dane O'Hara – with 20 internationals behind him. Nicknamed 'Fredman' because he says 'man' after everything, he had his Championship baptism in front of 18,000 Humberside fans in the local Derby against Hull Kingston Rovers at the Boulevard. Rovers won 23-8. Fred first came to the notice of British supporters after a sparkling tour in 1980. Hull made approaches then, but he chose to play grade football in Sydney for a while instead.

Harry Archer

Born: 'over 21', Workington, Cumbria, England.
Height: 5ft 8in.   *Weight:* 13st 7lb.
Position: Co-coach (with Bill Smith).
Club: Workington Town.
Club Honours
Challenge Cup: runners up 1957/58
Championship Play-off: runners up 1957/58.

Stand off Harry Archer was a great inspiration to the successful Workington Town side of the fifties. He topped a brilliant season in 1957/58 by gaining selection for the Australasia tour that summer. He played in eight matches on the tour, but never gained selection for the Tests. That disappointment followed the frustration of being a double 'bridesmaid' in domestic competition.

First there was only a runners up medal in the Challenge Cup final against Wigan, then followed a 20-3 defeat by Hull in the Championship Play-off before a crowd of nearly 60,000 at Odsal. In the Wembley match a high tackle by Wigan's Mick Sullivan laid him and he subsequently returned to finish the match in a semi-conscious state.

Harry's first coaching job came in May 1983 when he was appointed joint coach of Workington with Bill Smith. In their first year they gained promotion to the first division.

Chris Arkwright

Born: February 8, 1959, St Helens, Merseyside, England.
Height: 6ft 0in.   *Weight:* 13st 9lb.
Position: Stand off.
Club: St. Helens.
Great Britain Honours
Debut (under 24): January 1982 v France (in Leeds)
Appearances (under 24): one.
Club Honours
Lancashire Cup: runners up 1982/83.

Club top try scorer in the 1980/81 season, Chris is at home playing either at centre, second row, loose forward, or his favourite stand off position. A fitter at the nearby Bold Colliery, Chris has spent all his pro-

Chris Arkwright

fessional career at Knowsley Road like his father and grandfather before him. Unlucky with injuries, he would surely have otherwise added to his solitary Under 24 appearance. But on recent form, there is every reason to believe he will eventually win a full cap. Answering to the nickname 'Bernard' Chris enjoys fishing in his spare time in the company of his pet Great Dane.

Kevin Ashcroft

Born: June 5, 1944, Newton le
    Willows, Greater Manchester,
    England.
Height: 5ft 9in.   *Weight:* 14st 3lb.
Position: Manager/coach.
Club: Salford.
Great Britain Honours Debut (full):
    May 1968 v Australia (in Sydney
    – World Cup)
Appearances (full): five (one as sub).
Club Honours
 Challenge Cup: winners 1970/71
    (Leigh), 1973/74 (Warrington);
    runners up 1974/75 (Warrington)
John Player Trophy: winners 1973/
    74 (Warrington)
Lancashire Cup: winners 1970/71
    (Leigh), 1982/83 (Warrington –
    coach); runners up 1965/66
    (Rochdale) 1969/70 (Leigh)
BBC Floodlit Trophy: winners 1969/
    70 (Leigh), 1974/75
    (Warrington), 1976/77 (Leigh –
    player-coach)
Man of the Match Award: John
    Player Trophy final – 1973/74.

Kevin has spent a great deal of his career alongside Alex Murphy, so it is hardly surprising that he led Warrington to success in the Lancashire Cup in his first full season at Wilderspool.

He started his professional career in Yorkshire, joining Dewsbury from Leigh St. Mary's in 1962. It was at Leigh that he teamed up with Murphy for the first time, a move which heralded the best part of Kevin's playing career. Between then and the mid-seventies he appeared in three Challenge Cup finals at Wembley (winning two) and gained winners' medals in the Lancashire Cup, Floodlit Trophy, and the John Player Trophy. Kevin had one of his best games in the final of the John Player Trophy in 1974. By then he had moved to Warrington – following Murphy again – and his performance earned him the Man of the Match award. His first coaching appointment was with Leigh in 1975. But in August 1978 he teamed up with Alex Murphy again, becoming his assistant at Salford. Kevin, who made six Great Britain appearances, and played in two World Cup competitions in 1968 and 1970, joined Warrington as coach in November, 1980. He parted company with them at the end of the 1984 season and returned to Salford.

Ray Ashton

Born: October 26, 1960, Widnes,
    Cheshire, England.
Height: 5ft 8in.   *Weight:* 11st 4lb.
Position: Scrum half.
Club: Oldham.
Great Britain Honours
Debut (under 24): January 1983 v
    France (in Carpentras)
Appearances (under 24): three.
Club Honours
Division Two: winners 1981/82.

Although born in Widnes, it was Oldham who gave Ray his big break when they took him from local amateur Rugby League in 1978. He has proved himself a popular scrum half with the Watersheddings crowd, regularly scoring important tries. In their Second Division Championship year of 1981/82 he scored 26 tries including four in the 41-0 defeat of Huyton.

Ray gained his first Great Britain honours in the Under 24 International with France in January 1983, and in the game at Villeneuve the following November, he became

Ray Ashton

only the third player to score a hat trick of tries in England-France Under 24 matches. His decisive role earned him the Man of the Match award and subsequent selection for the 1984 senior tour. A wheel balancer by trade, Ray's pastimes are tennis, camping, astronomy, and crosswords.

John Atkinson

Born: October 30, 1946, Leeds, West Yorkshire, England.
Height: 6ft 0in.   *Weight:* 13st 0lb.
  Position: Coach.

Club: Carlisle.
Great Britain Honours
Debut (full): June 1968 v France (in Auckland – World Cup)
  Appearances (full): 26.
Club Honours
Division one: winners 1966/67, 1967/68, 1968/69, 1969/70, 1971/72 (all Leeds)
Challenge Cup: winners 1967/68, 1976/77, 1977/78 (all Leeds); runners up 1970/71, 1971/72 (both Leeds)
Premiership Trophy: winners 1974/75, 1978/79 (both Leeds)
John Player Trophy: winners 1972/73 (Leeds)
Championship Play-off: winners 1968/69, 1971/72 (both Leeds); runners up 1969/70, 1972/73 (both Leeds)
Yorkshire Cup: winners 1968/69, 1970/71, 1972/73, 1973/74, 1975/76, 1979/80, 1980/81 (all Leeds)
BBC Floodlit Trophy: winners 1970/71 (Leeds).

John had a remarkable playing career at Leeds, appearing in 20 major finals and winning 16 of them. A flying winger, John scored for Leeds in the majority of those finals and went over for tries in the 1968, 1977 and 1978 Challenge Cup finals. He is the only man to have scored tries in three different finals at Wembley. He is also the only English-born player to have headed the League's try scoring list three times since the war – in 1969/70, 1971/72 (shared with Mike Lamb) and 1972/73. One of Great Britain's most capped players, with 26 Tests and 12 tries, he toured with Great Britain three times and England once. He has also played in four World Cup competitions, gaining a winners' medal with Great Britain in 1972. He took over as player-coach at Carlisle in February 1983 in succession to Mick Morgan. It was too late to save the club from relegation and 1983/84 saw John in Second Division rugby for the first time. After a serious injury that season, John decided to retire as a player and concentrate on coaching. His former occupations have included G.P.O. engineer, carpenter and joiner, and police officer. As a youngster, he represented Leeds City at athletics and boxing. Now he enjoys a game of golf or reading.

Ian Ball

Born: June 26, 1954, St. Helens, Merseyside, England.
Height: 5ft 8in.   *Weight:* 11st 2lb. Position: Centre.
Club: Barrow.
Club Honours
Division Two: winners 1983/84
John Player Trophy: runners up 1980/81
Lancashire Cup: winners 1983/84.

This former Waterloo, Wasps, and England under 24 Rugby Union player, joined Barrow in October 1978. He scored a try on his debut against Leeds and has continued to register points for the club ever since. He scored a club record 305 in the 1979/80 season to earn a place in the record books alongside his father, the late Joe Ball, who starred for the club in the 1950's and still holds the record for the most goals in one season – 135. Of all the points Ian has scored none have been more important than the three goals and one dropped goal he landed in the 1983/84 Lancashire Cup final in which Barrow beat Widnes, producing one of the biggest upsets in

recent Rugby League. The Cumbrians became the first Second Division side to win the trophy. In 1981 Ian gave a brilliant performance in the semi-final of the John Player Trophy to help take Barrow to their first final for 14 years. His appearance in the final created a record; he became the first person to play in the John Player final under both codes, League and Union.

Maurice Bamford

Born: April 20, 1936, Leeds, West Yorkshire, England.
Height: 5ft 10in.   *Weight: 15st 0lb. Position: Coach*
Club: Leeds.
Club Honours
John Player Special Trophy: winners 1983/84 (Leeds – coach)
Yorkshire Cup: runners up 1979/80 (Halifax – coach).

Few men have seen both sides of Rugby League as starkly as Maurice. In 1977 he was assistant coach to Peter Fox at Bradford Northern and moved to take over as full coach to the financially moribund Halifax club. They were struggling for survival but Maurice, one of the best motivators in the game, set about restoring their pride. He chased around the West Yorkshire clubs picking up players for bargain prices, including both stand off Mick Blacker and goalkicking full-back Jimmy Birts from his former club, Northern. Amazingly, the club's playing fortunes swung round and they were promoted back to the First Division. Maurice, never a man to shirk a challenge, moved on to neighbours Huddersfield, who were also desperately trying to restore their former glories. But the

Fartown job went badly and, under a cloud of acrimony, Maurice switched across the Pennines in a shock appointment as Wigan coach. That move, too, ended in disappointment and Maurice returned to Yorkshire to take over at Bramley. Again disaster!After financial crises he left the McLaren Field club during the early part of 1983/84. Things looked grim for Maurice... then, out of the blue, he landed the plum job as Leeds coach in November 1983. Within a few months he had steered them to the John Player Special Trophy, and the Challenge Cup semi-final.

John Basnett

Born: January 3, 1957, Wallasey, Merseyside, England.
Height: 6ft 1in.   *Weight:* 12st 0lb.
Position: Winger.
Club: Widnes.
Great Britain Honours
Debut (full): February 1984 v France (in Leeds) Appearances (full): one.
Club Honours
Challenge Cup: winners 1983/84; runners up 1981/82
Premiership Trophy: winners 1981/82, 1982/83
Lancashire Cup: runners up 1983/84.

Widnes had no hesitation in signing former England Under 23 Rugby Union International John Basnett from New Brighton RUFC in April 1981. They had just watched him score five tries in an A team trial. He soon adapted to the new code and a couple of months after his Widnes debut he was scoring another five in a John Player Trophy match with Hunslet. This feat equalled John Joyner's Competition record and also the Widnes club record for the most tries in one game – held jointly with Eddie Cunningham.

John finished that season as the club's top try scorer with 26, a figure that also put him in third place in the League list. He managed five tries from his 23 appearances in the 1982/83 season, but fought his way back the following season as he tussled with Joe Lydon for the honour of being top try scorer for the club. His revived try scoring feats after injury blows won him his first Great Britain selection in the first Test against France at Headingley in 1984. Although he was not selected for the 1984 tour, he was flown out as a replacement for the injured Ronnie Duane.

Graham Beale

Born: August 5, 1954, Castleford, West Yorkshire, England.
Height: 5ft 6in.   *Weight:* 11st 0lb.
Position: Half back.
Club: Keighley.
Club Honours
Leading goals and points scorer: 1980/81, 1981/82, 1982/83, (all with Keighley).

A former winger, Graham moved to Keighley from Doncaster, and in his five years with the club has kicked more than 400 goals. He was leading goalscorer and points scorer in the three seasons up to 1983/84. But he did not have too happy a time last season following a series of injuries and a spell in dispute with the Lawkholme Lane club.

Kevin Beardmore

Born: June 21, 1960, Castleford, West Yorkshire, England.

Kevin Beardmore

Height: 5ft 7in.   *Weight:* 12st 10lb.
Position: Hooker.
Club: Castleford.

Kevin took some time to establish himself in the Castleford side. He signed professional forms in 1977, but played only 18 matches in his first three seasons. In 1982/83 he finally settled himself as the regular hooker, scoring 16 tries. His best performance came in the 66-8 trouncing of Carlisle in April 1983, when he scored four tries. It was a memorable day all round for the Beardmore family because his club mate and brother Bob kicked 12 goals and scored a try to give him 27 points – just two short of the First Division record. He was selected for the Great Britain tour down under in 1984. Along with Leigh's Steve Donlan, he was the only member of the party with no international experience.

Robert Beardmore
Born: June 21, 1960, Castleford,
   West Yorkshire, England.
Height: 5ft 6in.   *Weight:* 11st 9lb.
Position: Scrum Half.
Club: Castleford.
Club Honours
Premiership Trophy: runners up
   1983/84 Yorkshire Cup: winners
   1981/82; runners up 1983/84.

Having gone close to breaking the first division scoring record in the 1982/83 season, when he was just two points short of the necessary 29 in one game, Castleford's Bob Beardmore made it his own in October 1983. Three tries and 11 goals gave him 34 points in a championship game with Leeds, to shatter John Wood's old mark by six points. Bob followed brother Kevin to Castleford in 1978 and replaced Gary Stephens as scrum half in 1980/81 – his first full season, in which he scored 17 tries. It is his goalkicking, however, that has brought him to the fringe of international honours, particularly in 1982/83 when he kicked 117 goals to put him fourth on the list. During the season he twice kicked 10 goals in a match. He crowned another memorable season in 1983/84 by being the league's joint leading goalkicker with Steve Hesford. At the same time he broke Sammy Lloyd's club record for the most points in a season.

Dean Bell

Born: April 29, 1962, Auckland, New Zealand.
Height: 5ft 11in.   *Weight:* 13st 2lb.
Position: Centre.
Club: Leeds.
New Zealand Honours
Debut (full): June 1983 v Australia (in Auckland)
Appearances (full): three.
Club Honours
John Player Special Trophy: winners 1983/84 (Leeds).

Still 22, New Zealand international Dean has made a big impression at Headingley since joining Leeds in November, 1983. He scored on his Leeds debut in the John Player Special Trophy win over Hull KR and a couple of months later was a member of the side which lifted that trophy, beating Widnes in the final. Dean's arrival at Headingley coincided with the appointment of coach Maurice Bamford and soon afterwards the club went through one of the best unbeaten runs in their history with 18 successive matches without defeat. Carlisle was Dean's first port of call in this country when he joined the Cumbrians along with brother Ian, and Clayton Friend in

August 1982. In his one campaign at Brunton Park he scored 11 tries in 23 games to make him the second highest try scorer for the club that season. He also represented Cumbria against the touring Australians.

He returned to Auckland, at the end of the season, to play with Manukau, but the following November came back to join Leeds. He made his New Zealand international debut in the first Test against Australia at Carlaw Park, Auckland, in June 1983. The match was New Zealand's Jubilee Test – marking 75 years of rugby league in the country.

Billy Benyon

Born: March 7, 1945, St. Helens, Merseyside, England.
Height: 5ft 10in.   *Weight:* 12st 11lb.
Position: Coach.
Club: St. Helens.
Great Britain Honours
Debut (full): February 1971 v France (in Toulouse)
Appearances (full): five (one as sub).
Club Honours
Division one: winners 1964/65, 1965/66, 1974/75 (all St. Helens)
Challenge Cup: winners 1965/66, 1971/72, 1975/76 (all St. Helens)
Premiership Trophy: winners 1975/76, 1976/77 (both St. Helens)
John Player Trophy: winners 1977/78 (Warrington – player/coach) winners 1980/81 (Warrington – coach); runners up 1978/79 (Warrington – player/coach)
Championship Play-off: winners 1965/66, 1969/70, 1970/71 (all St. Helens)
Lancashire Cup: winners 1962/63, 1964/65, 1967/68, 1968/69 (all St.

Billy Benyon

Helens) 1980/81 (Warrington –
coach); runners up 1970/71 (St.
Helens) 1982/83 (St. Helens –
coach)
BBC Floodlit Trophy: winners 1971/
72, 1975/76 (both St. Helens);
runners up 1965/66, 1968/69,
1970/71 (all St. Helens)
Award: Trumanns Man of Steel
Coach of the Year – 1980/81.

The return of Billy Benyon to Knowsley Road as coach in 1982 was
welcomed by the St. Helens supporters who remembered with relish
the performances he gave for the
club in his playing days. At centre
or stand off, Billy played his heart
out for his beloved Saints and won
virtually every honour with them.
He appeared in 18 major finals with
St. Helens, including three winning
Challenge Cups at Wembley. A
joiner, Billy signed for St. Helens on
his 16th birthday in 1961 and won
his first honour 18 months later
when he was in the side that lifted
the Lancashire Cup. As a schoolboy,
he captained the St. Helens and

Lancashire teams in 1959, but the
following year he turned his atten-
tions to soccer. Just as talented at
the round ball game, he won County
honours in 1960 and had trials with
Bolton Wanderers and West Brom.
He turned down an offer to join West
Brom because of his preference for
rugby league.
He represented Great Britain six
times in 1971 and 1972, but was
never selected to tour. After 15
years at Knowsley Road, Billy took
his experience to nearby Warrington in 1977 and during his first
season at Wilderspool he won a John
Player Trophy winners medal – the
one which had eluded him at St.
Helens. He was appointed coach and
under his leadership the club
reached two more John Player finals
and a Lancashire Cup final before
he was sacked in March 1982. Billy
took the club to an Industrial
Tribunal and won his case. Two
months out of the game, he was
offered the coach's job at Saints and
during his first year in charge took
them to the Lancashire Cup final,
where they were beaten by Warrington. Billy has now blended a fine
mixture of youth and experience
into the St. Helens team. They
showed their potential towards the
end of the 1983/84 season and could
be the team to watch in 1984/85.

John Bevan
Born: October 28, 1950, Tylorstown,
Rhondda, South Wales.
Height: 6ft 0in.   *Weight:* 13st 9lb.
Position: Winger/Centre.
Club: Warrington.
Great Britain Honours
Debut (full): June 1974 v Australia
(in Brisbane)
Appearances (full): six.

Club Honours
Challenge Cup: winners 1973/4;
  runners up 1974/75
Premiership Trophy: runners up
  1976/77
John Player Trophy: winners 1973/
  74, 1977/78, 1980/81
Lancashire Cup: winners 1980/81,
  1982/83
Club Championship: winners 1973/ 74.

Hailing from Tylorstown in the Rhondda – home of former world flyweight boxing champion Jimmy Wilde – John Bevan has been a credit to his country at both rugby codes. While with Cardiff RU Club, he toured New Zealand with the British Lions in 1971 and gained ten Welsh caps.

His switch to the professional game in 1973, when he joined Warrington, saw him win further international honours with six appearances for Great Britain and 17 for Wales. He toured Australia in 1974, and was in the Welsh team for the 1975 World Championships. Injury ruled him out of the 1979 Great Britain tour after gaining selection. A P.E. teacher at the Arnold School, Blackpool, John had his benefit in 1983 after ten years with Warrington. It was richly deserved, for with Bevan's muscular pace Warrington enjoyed one of their most successful periods ever. They became the only team to win the John Player Trophy three times and John scored tries in each of those victories. Significantly, he missed their only other appearance in the final – when they lost to Widnes.

Two Wembley appearances in the Challenge Cup have highlighted John's memorable career. A winners medal came his way in 1974 follow-ing a 24-9 win over Featherstone, and the next year he was back. This time Warrington lost to Widnes in an all-Cheshire final – even though John scored the game's opening try. But it was John's semi-final performance that will be remembered, when he scored a hat trick of tries in the 11-4 win defeat of Leeds. A qualified lifeguard, John is also a recognised athletics coach, a fair squash player and an accomplished horse rider.

Jimmy Birts
Born: September 13, 1956,
  Bradford, West Yorkshire,
  England.
Height: 6ft 0in.   *Weight:* 12st 4lb.
Position: Full back.
Club: Carlisle.
Club Honours
Leading goalkicker: 1978/79, 1979/
  80, 1980/81 (all at Halifax).

Leading goalkicker at Halifax in the three successive seasons between 1979 and 1981, Jimmy's totals of 86, 97 and 100 were sufficient to put him into the League's leading ten kickers each time. Yorkshireman Jimmy began with Bradford North-ern and then moved to Halifax, where his kicking ability caught the eye of Wigan. They paid £22,000 for him in June 1981, but he was una-ble to settle and after only 12 games in 12 months he moved North to Carlisle for £10,000.

Tommy Bishop
Born: October 15, 1940, St. Helens,
  Merseyside, England.
Height: 5ft 4in.   *Weight:* 11st 0lb.
Position: Coach.
Club: Unattached.
Great Britain Honours

Debut (full): June 1966 v Australia
(in Sydney)
Appearances (full): 15.
Club Honours
Challenge Cup: winners 1965/66
(St. Helens)
Championship Play-off: winners
1965/66 (St. Helens); runners up
1966/67 (St. Helens)
Lancashire Cup: winners 1967/68,
1968/69 (both St. Helens)
BBC Floodlit Trophy: runners up
1968/69 (St. Helens).

After 12 years coaching in Australia, Tommy was lured back to Britain in November 1980 as coach to Workington Town. Four months after the appointment he was made the club's first full time General Manager. He remained at Workington until June 1982 – resigning shortly after guiding the club back to the First Division. He rested for a while, running the Central Hotel in Keswick but after 12 months he was tempted back, to join Leigh as coach. He quit in June 1984 after a disagreement over changes in his backroom staff. Tommy runs a public house in the St. Helens area.

As a player, Tommy began at Blackpool Borough, but it was at St. Helens that Tommy made his mark on the game, highlighted by his try in the 1966 Challenge Cup final victory over Wigan. 'Saints' won the Championship Play-off the same season and Tommy's scrum half performance earned him selection for the Great Britain tour that summer. He made his Great Britain Test debut in the first Test with Australia in Sydney.

Mick Blacker
Born: July 30, 1948, Barnsley,

South Yorkshire, England.
Height: 5ft 6in   *Weight:* 12st 0lb.
Position: Coach.
Club: Mansfield.
Club Honours
Division Two: winners 1973/74
(Bradford Northern)
Challenge Cup: runners up 1972/73
(Bradford Northern)
John Player Trophy: winners 1974/
75 (Bradford Northern)
Yorkshire Cup: runners up 1979/80
(Halifax).

If honesty and maximum effort alone won trophies then Mick Blacker would have obtained more than most. Nearing the end of a long career, Mick has given 100% at all his clubs – Bradford Northern, Halifax and, more recently, Warrington. Mick joined Northern from a Huddersfield youth side Birkby Youth Club and gave ten years' loyal service to the Odsal team and their supporters.

One of the moments he will cherish from his Bradford days was his one and only appearance at Wembley. Sadly for Mick and his colleagues they could not match the fire power of a strong Featherstone side that day, and were flattened 33-14. He was a member of the Bradford side which won the second division title in 1973/74, and the John Player Trophy the following year. He moved to help revive struggling Halifax in 1977. By 1979/80 they had gained promotion from the Second Division and reached the Yorkshire Cup final where they gave First Division Leeds a good game before going down 15-6.

Mick became Halifax coach in June 1980, holding the post for two years before moving on to Warrington in January 1983. Attempting a second spell at coaching, Mick accepted the post at newly-formed Mansfield in May 1984. Mick's brother Brian is on the playing staff at Huddersfield.

Reg Bowden

Born: December 17, 1949, Widnes, Cheshire, England.
Height: 5ft 8in. *Weight:* 12st 0lb.
Position: Player/coach.
Club: Warrington.
Club Honours
First Division: winners 1977/78 (Widnes)
Second Division: winners 1982/83 (Fulham)
Challenge Cup: winners 1974/75 , 1978/79 (both Widnes); runners up 1975/76, 1976/77 (both Widnes)
Premiership Trophy: winners 1979/ 80 (Widnes) runners up 1977/78 (Widnes)
John Player Trophy: winners 1975/ 76, 1978/79 (both Widnes); runners up 1974/75, 1977/78, 1979/80 (all Widnes)
Lancashire Cup: winners 1974/75, 1975/76, 1976/77, 1978/79, 1979/ 80, (all Widnes); runners up 1971/ 72 (Widnes)
Man of the Match Award: John Player Cup Final 1975/76
BBC Floodlit Trophy: winners 1978/ 79 (Widnes); runners up 1973/74 (Widnes).

Born and bred in Widnes, Reg remains a firm favourite in the town - even though he defected to the South. Reg was the first signing by Fulham as player-coach, on their acceptance into the Rugby League in July 1980. The choice proved to be a shrewd one. In their first season Fulham were promoted to the First Division, and although they came straight back down again, the experience did them no harm. They gained their second stint in the top flight in 1983/84, having won the Second Division title the previous year, and although they still languished in the bottom half of the table, Reg led his men to some impressive victories.

Before moving to Fulham, Reg spent all his career at Widnes, first playing for the under 11's, under 16's, and then the senior side. He made 19 appearances in major finals, 11 of them on the winning side. His talents as a scrum half are

Reg Bowden

supplemented by his qualities as a leader, and both were illustrated in the 1975/76 John Player Trophy final. Reg not only captained the Widnes team with rare fire, but his personal tally of one try and a drop goal earned him the Man of the Match award.

In all his leadership took Widnes to four Challenge Cup finals within five years – with two victories. International rugby has eluded him, but he is regarded as one of the greatest uncapped scrum halves of his day. Reg's benefit season of 1978/79 raised £17,000. In the 1984 close season, Reg retired from playing and returned to his native Cheshire to take up the post of coach at Warrington.

Dennis Boyd

Born: September 1, 1950, Wigan, Greater Manchester, England.
Height: 5ft 11in.   *Weight:* 14st 10lb.
Position: Loose forward/prop.
Club: Salford.
Club Honours
Division Two: winners 1977/78 (Leigh)
BBC2 Floodlit Trophy: runners up 1976/77 (Leigh).

Between January 1983 and January 1984, Dennis saw service with four clubs – Carlisle, Swinton, Oldham and Salford, the middle two on loan. The much-travelled forward began his career with Wigan in 1973.
They got rid of him and he went playing local amateur rugby where he was spotted by Leigh, who snapped him up for a nominal fee. A great tackler who can play at loose forward or prop, he enjoyed some of his best games while at Hilton Park and was a member of the Leigh

team beaten by Castleford in the 1976/77 Floodlit final.

After five years with Leigh he moved back to Wigan who this time had to fork out £9,000. He was a member of the Wigan team relegated at the end of the 1979/80 season and, after coming back up with them the following season, he returned to the Second Division with the newly formed Carlisle team. Once again he was a member of a promotion winning team. After that he failed to gain a regular spot in the Carlisle team and he sought two loan spells, first at Swinton then Oldham, before securing a permanent transfer to Salford during the 1983/84 season.

Mark Broadhurst

Born: April 8, 1955, Christchurch, New Zealand.
Height: 6ft 0in.   *Weight:* 15st 7lb.
Position: Prop forward.
Club: Hull Kingston Rovers.
New Zealand Honours
Debut (full): 1979 v Great Britain
Appearances (full): 17.
Club Honours
Division One: winners 1983/84
Premiership Trophy: winners 1983/84.

Kiwi Mark played Sydney first grade football as a highly rated prop forward for first Manly-Warringah and then Illawarra. Originally with Auckland, he gained his first international honours in 1979 against Great Britain. Mark joined Hull Kingston Rovers in September 1983, and won the Man of the Match award on his debut.

Mark Broadhurst

John Buckton

Born: November 9, 1962, Leeds,
West Yorkshire, England.
Height: 5ft 8in.   *Weight:* 12st 0lb.
Position: Stand off.
Club: Doncaster.
Club Honours
Leading scorer: 1981/82, 1982/83,
1983/84 (joint).

A bargain £500 buy from Hunslet in 1979, John Buckton has not stopped breaking records since. During the 1980/81 season he scored 17 tries to equal Brian Wriglesworth's 23-year-old club record (the 17th came in the final match of the season at Craven Cottage to make him the first visiting player to score a hat trick at Fulham). The following year John scored 18... starting with four in the opening match against Rochdale. That burst came in the middle of a remarkable sequence. He had scored in five successive Division Two games at the end of the previous season and proceeded to score in the first four League games of 1981/82 to make it nine in a row –

just one short of Roger Millwards Second Division record.

In 1982/83 John scored 18 tries again. The figure could have been significantly higher as he missed the early part of the season, and also went on a month's loan to Wakefield Trinity. His first try of the season did not come until 21st November. In February 1984, he was on loan again, this time to Dewsbury.

Arthur Bunting

Born: June 13, 1936, Ackworth,
West Yorkshire, England.
Height: 5ft 5in.   *Weight:* 12st 7lb.
Position: Team Manager.
Club: Hull.
Club Honours
Division one: winners 1982/83 (Hull
– coach) Division two: winners
1978/79 (Hull – coach)
Challenge Cup: winners 1981/82
(Hull – coach); runners up 1963/
64 (Hull KR) 1979/80, 1982/83
(both as Hull coach)
Premiership Trophy: runners up
1980/81, 1981/82, 1982/83 (all as
Hull coach)
John Player Trophy: winners 1981/
82 (Hull – coach)
Yorkshire Cup: winners 1966/67
(Hull KR) 1982/83, 1983/84 (both
as Hull coach)
BBC Floodlit Trophy: winners 1979/
80 (Hull – coach)
Awards: Trumanns Man of Steel,
Coach of the Year – 1982 and
1983.

Arthur is the most successful coach of the eighties. He took over at Second Division Hull in January 1978, steered them to promotion the next season, and to at least one major final every year since. That sequence of success comprises three

Challenge Cup Finals, three consecutive Premiership Trophy finals, a John Player Trophy victory, two Yorkshire Cup wins, and a Floodlit final success. Not surprisingly, Arthur was Coach of the Year in 1982 and 1983.

Trophies were not so easy to come by when Arthur was a scrum half with Hull Kingston Rovers in the sixties. But he was a member of the Rovers team beaten by Widnes in the 1964 Challenge Cup final. The pressures at Hull took their toll during the 1983/84 season and ill-health forced Arthur to take a six-week break.

Mick Burke

Born: September 25, 1958, St.
  Helens, Merseyside, England.
Height: 5ft 11in. *Weight:* 14st 10lb.
Position: Full back.
Club: Widnes.
Great Britain Honours
Debut (full): November 1980 v New
  Zealand (in Leeds) (under 24):
  November 1979 v France (in
  Leigh)
Appearances (full): three (one as
  sub)
  (under 24): five.
Club Honours
Challenge Cup: winners 1978/79,
  1980/81, 1983/84; runners up
  1981/82
Premiership Trophy: winners 1979/
  80, 1981/82, 1982/83
John Player Trophy: winners 1978/
  79; runners up 1979/80, 1983/84
Lancashire Cup: winners 1978/79,
  1979/80; runners up 1981/82,
  1983/84
BBC Floodlit Trophy: winners 1978/
  79
Man of the Match Awards: Lance
  Todd Award – 1981; Challenge

Cup Final; Harry Sunderland Trophy – 1982; Premiership Trophy.

In 1982 Mick joined the St. Helens pair Geoff Pimblett and George Nicholls as the only players to have won the Lance Todd Award and Harry Sunderland Trophy – the Man of the Match awards in the Challenge Cup final and Premiership Trophy final respectively. The Lance Todd award came first – in 1981 following his performance in Widnes's Challenge Cup final win over Hull KR, in which he scored the opening try, kicked four goals, and was instrumental in Mick George's decisive try. A year later Mick added the Harry Sunderland Trophy, when he kicked four goals, scored a great solo try, and assisted in two other tries.

A great fighter, and consistent goalkicker, Mick joined Widnes from Waterloo RUFC on 16th May 1978. His career in the 15-a-side code had been successful. With schoolboy honours at under 15, under 16, and under 19 and an appearance for the England under 23 'B' team. Mick made his Widnes debut in the Lancashire Cup tie against Huyton on August 20, 1978 and scored a try. During that first season he set two club records which still stand: 140 goals and 316 points. But despite being the club's top goalscorer every season since 1978/79, he has never topped the League's goalscoring list. His 140 in the 1978/79 season gave him his best place, third.

Mick started his international career with goals, four on his under 24 debut against France in 1979 and two on his first full appearance in 1980. He reached a personal milestone during the 1982/83 season when he kicked his 500th goal for Widnes and scored his 1000th point. In 1984 he was selected for the tour of Australasia.

Tony Burke

Born: August 25, 1961, Leeds, West Yorkshire, England.
Height: 6ft 0in.   *Weight:* 16st 0lb.
    Position: Prop forward.
Club: St. Helens.
Club Honours
John Player Trophy: runners up 1982/83 (Leeds).

Tony joined St. Helens in 1983 after spending one and a half seasons with Leeds. A prop forward, he won his only piece of silverware in senior rugby league during his stay in Headingley, when he played in the final of the John Player Trophy during the 1982/83 season. Leeds were on the wrong end of a 15-4 scoreline to Wigan.

One of Tony's best games was in the match against the visiting Kangaroos of 1982. Although he was on the losing side with Leeds, his performance earned him the Man of the Match award.

Chris Burton

Born: October 5, 1956, Leeds, West Yorkshire, England.
Height: 6ft 2in.   *Weight:* 15st 0lb.
Position: Second row forward.
Club: Hull Kingston Rovers.
Great Britain Honours
Debut (full): November 1982 v Australia (in Wigan)
Appearances (full): one.
Club Honours
Division One: winners 1983/84 (Hull KR)
Challenge Cup: runners up 1980/81

Tony Burke

(Hull KR)
Premiership Trophy: winners 1980/81, 1983/84 (both Hull KR)
John Player Trophy: runners up 1981/82 (Hull KR)
Yorkshire Cup: winners 1976/77 (Leeds).

A former Great Britain Colts player, Chris joined his home town team, Leeds, when he was 17. His first honour came in 1976 when he was a member of the side which beat Featherstone 16-12 in the Yorkshire Cup final.

Chris was not a regular first team choice after that, and he welcomed the move to Huddersfield for the start of the 1978/79 season. That first season at Fartown saw the team bottom of the First Division, and the next year, further disaster, as Huddersfield finished third from bottom of the Second Division.

Chris must have wondered what the future held and was as surprised as everbody else when Hull KR signed him for £18,000 just before the Cup transfer deadline, in February 1981. Not only was he eligible to play for Rovers in the Cup, he went all the way to Wembley with them, scoring the final try in their 18-9 defeat by Widnes. Compensation came his way a week later when Rovers beat Hull in the Premiership Trophy final.

Some impressive performances in 1982 led to Chris being selected for the second Test with the 'invincible' Kangaroos at Wigan. He was selected for the Great Britain training team in 1984.

David Cairns

David Cairns

Born: March 1, 1959, Barrow in
  Furness, Cumbria, England.
Height: 5ft 4in.   *Weight:* 10st 8lb.
Position: Scrum half.
Club: Barrow.
Great Britain Honours
Debut (full): January 1984 v France
  (in Avignon)
  (under 24): November 1979 v
  France (in Leigh)
Appearances (full): two
  (under 24): two.
Club Honours
Division Two: winners 1983/84
Lancashire Cup: winners 1983/84
John Player Cup: runners up 1980/
  81
Man of the Match: 1983/84
  (Lancashire Cup final)
Awards: Greenalls Man of Steel
  Second Division Player of the
  Year, 1983/84.

Scrum half David has spent all his professional career with his home town club, Barrow, and in 1983 played one of the best matches of his life to help his side beat favourites Widnes in the final of the Lancashire Cup. His performance earned him the Man of the Match award. David toured with the Great Britain under 18 side in 1977 and, two years later, made his under 24 debut against France at Leigh. However, his second under 24 appearance did not come until almost two and a half years later.

Since then his game has improved and in 1984 saw him make his first full international appearance, against France at Avignon in January – the only Second Division player in the team. His season ended with him collecting the Greenalls Man of Steel Second Division Player of the year award.

Danny Campbell

Born: 1958, Auckland, New
   Zealand.
Height: 6ft 0in.   *Weight:* 15st 10lb.
Position: Prop forward.
Club: Wigan.
Club Honours
John Player Trophy: winners 1982/
   83.

New Zealander Danny joined Wigan
from Far North Falcons in October
1980. He played only 12 games in
his debut season, scoring his first
try against Rochdale Hornets in
January 1981.
   Danny's great asset is his fierce
competitive attitude which was
demonstrated in the John Player
Trophy semi final against Warrington in 1982/83. His non-stop performance helped Wigan through to the
final and gained him the Man of the
Match award. Danny gave a similar
display in the final, in which Wigan
beat Leeds, and was again a can-
didate for Man of the Match, which
went to team mate Martin Foy. The
mainstay of the team for two
seasons, he missed Wigan's 1984
Wembley appearance after being
out for most of the year with a badly
broken ankle.

Brian Case

Born: January 14, 1958, St. Helens,
   Merseyside, England.
Height: 5ft 11in.   *Weight:* 14st 7lb.
Position: Prop forward
Club: Wigan.
Great Britain Honours
Debut (under 24): January 1979 v
   France (in Limoux)
Appearances (under 24): three (one
   as sub).
Club Honours
Challenge Cup: runners up 1983/84

(Wigan)
Premiership Trophy: runners up
   1976/77 (Warrington)
John Player Trophy: winners 1980/
   81 (Warrington) 1982/83 (Wigan);
   runners up 1978/79 (Warrington)
Lancashire Cup: winners 1980/81
   (Warrington).

Brian established himself as a
talented prop with Warrington but
quit them in protest after a dispute.
A loan to Salford was in the offing,
but Wigan stepped in to buy him
just before the Cup transfer deadline in January 1983, and a week
later he was appearing in the John
Player Trophy final. He came on as
substitute for Graeme West as
Wigan caused a stir by beating
Leeds to give Brian his second winners medal in the competition.
   He had won his first with Warrington two years earlier. He joined
Warrington from Blackbrook, St.
Helens, ARL side in 1975. He has
four under 24 appearances to his
credit, and one England appearance.
His under 24 debut came against
France in 1979, and his England
debut two years later.
   The 1983/84 season was a
memorable one for Brian. He played
in Wigan's losing Challenge Cup
final side at Wembley and was then
selected for the senior Great Britain
squad to tour Down Under in the
summer.

Len Casey

Born: January 28, 1950, Hull,
   Humberside, England.
Height: 5ft 11in.   *Weight:* 15st 0lb.
Position: Prop forward.
Club: Hull Kingston Rovers.
Great Britain Honours
Debut (full): June 1977 v France

(Auckland – World Cup)
Appearances (full): 12 (two as sub).
Club Honours
Division One: winners 1983/84
(Hull KR)
Challenge Cup: winners 1979/80
(Hull KR); runners up 1980/81
(Hull KR)
Premiership Trophy: winners 1980/
81 (Hull KR); runners up 1978/79
(Bradford Northern)
John Player Trophy: winners 1979/
80 (Bradford Northern); runners
up 1981/82 (Hull KR)
Yorkshire Cup: runners up 1980/81
(Hull KR)
BBC2 Floodlit Trophy: winners
1977/78 (Hull KR)
Man of the Match awards: 1979/80
John Player Trophy final; Harry
Sunderland Trophy 1980/81 –
Premiership final.

At one stage in Len's career, it
looked as if he was going to carry
around one of those unwanted 'unlucky' tags. For in January 1979 he
left Hull KR to join Bradford Northern and three months later Rovers
won the First Division title.

In January 1980 he returned to
Hull KR and Bradford Northern
won the First Division title three
months later. Born and bred in Hull,
Len joined the 'Airlie Birds' in 1968
and stayed with them until 1975,
when he moved across the city to
Rovers in a £6,000 deal. He helped
them win the BBC2 Floodlit Trophy
in 1977 defeating St. Helens in the
final; and gained a Great Britain
World Cup place.

A £25,000 transfer took him
across Yorkshire to Bradford Northern in 1979. In the 12 months he
spent there he played in their winning John Player Trophy team and
was on the losing side in the

Premiership Trophy final. During
that period at Odsal he toured Down
Under with the Great Britain team
in 1979. Len moved back to Humberside after a year in Bradford, resigning for Rovers in January 1980
for a then record £38,000 fee. The
return to Rovers worked well for
both Len and the team. They went
on to successive Challenge Cup final
appearances in 1980 and 1981. John
Player and Yorkshire Cup final
appearances also followed, and in
1981 the Premiership Trophy final,
in which Len won the Harry Sunderland award as Man of the Match.

Still going strong, Len was selected for his third tour in 1984, but
had to miss it when suspension put
him out of action from May to
November. A publican, Len enjoys
reading and going for long walks.

Garry Clark

Born: January 4, 1965, Malta.
Height: 6ft 0in.   *Weight:* 12st 2lb.
Position: Winger.
Club: Hull Kingston Rovers.
Great Britain Honours
Debut (full): January 1984 v France
(in Avignon)
(under 24): January 1983 v
France (in Carpentras)
Appearances (full): two
(under 24): three.
Club Honours
Division One: winners 1983/84
Premiership Trophy: winners 1983/
84.

What a memorable first season
young Garry had with Hull Kingston Rovers in 1982/83. The former
Hull, Yorkshire and England
schoolboy player toured with Great
Britain Colts to Papua New Guinea
and Australia in 1982 and, upon his

Garry Clark

Club Honours
Division One: winners 1978/79
(Hull KR) 1979/80 (Bradford N)
1981/82 (Leigh)
Challenge Cup: winners 1970/71
(Leigh)
Premiership Trophy: runners up
1979/80 (Bradford N)
Championship Play-off: winners
1966/67 (Wakefield T)
BBC Floodlit Trophy: runners up
1979/80 (Hull KR)
Lancashire Cup: winners 1970/71,
1981/82 (both Leigh)
Yorkshire Cup: winners 1973/74
(Leeds).

With more clubs to his name than
Jack Nicklaus, Geoff made the 12th
move of his career in 1984 when he
joined Featherstone. A former Yorkshire County Rugby Union player,
he joined Wakefield Trinity in 1966.
The first of his many honours came
at the end of that first season as he
was in the Trinity side which beat
St. Helens (after a replay) to win the
Championship Play-off for the first
time in their history.

He has gone on to win the
Challenge Cup with Leigh and the
First Division championship three
times in four seasons – with Hull
Kingston Rovers, Bradford Nor-
thern and Leigh. He has also played
for Warrington, Leeds, York,
Bramley, and Oldham.

return, made his senior debut for
Rovers in the Championship match
with Workington on August 22. He
scored the seventh of his side's tries
in the 33-10 rout. Three days later,
Garry scored a hat trick against
Halifax. Altogether that season he
landed 17 tries to make him joint
top try scorer for the club (with Gary
Prohm).

The Great Britain selectors
drafted him into the under 24 team
for the match at Carpentras against
France – just five months after his
club debut and he bagged three
more. He made his full international debut in January 1984 and
was selected for the tour of Australasia that year.

Geoff Clarkson
Born: 1948, Wakefield, West
Yorkshire, England.
Height: 6ft 2in.   *Weight:* 15st 2lb.
Position: Prop/second row.
Club: Featherstone Rovers.

Mike Coulman
Born: May 6, 1944, Stafford, Staffs,
England.
Height: 6ft 1in.   *Weight:* 17st 0lb.
Position: Coach.
Club: Unattached.
Great Britain Honours
Debut (full): March 1971 v France
(in St. Helens)

Appearances (full): two (one as sub).
Club Honours
Division one: winners 1973/74,
　1975/76 (Salford)
Challenge Cup: runners up 1968/69
　(Salford)
Premiership Trophy: runners up
　1975/76 (Salford)
Lancashire Cup: runners up 1974/75
　(Salford)
BBC Floodlit final: winners 1974/75
　(Salford)
Man of the Match award:
　Lancashire Cup final – 1974/75.

A former Staffordshire policeman,
Mike made his name as a forward
with Moseley Rugby Union side. He
played for England nine times in
1967 and 1968 and toured South
Africa with the British Lions in
1968, playing in one of the four
Internationals. At the end of that
Lions tour, he considered the move
to the professional game and joined
Salford in October.

A second row prop forward, he
gave some memorable performances
for his pro club, none better than in
the 1974 Lancashire Cup final
against Widnes. Despite ending up
on the losing side, his non-stop performance earned him the first ever
Man of the Match award in the
competition. Mike made three Great
Britain appearances, all in 1971.
His debut was as substitute against
France at St. Helens. The other substitute also making his Great
Britain debut that day was David
Watkins – Mike's Salford team
mate.

A four year gap followed before
Mike gained more international re-
cognition for England in the 1975
World Championships. He started
coaching at Salford in succession to
Mal Aspey in 1983, but the Reds

were relegated at the end of that
season and Salford and Mike parted
company after nearly 16 years.
Mike was Midland Police heavyweight boxing champion in 1964
and 1965 and Staffordshire Police
100 and 220 yards sprint champion
in 1967.

David Creasser
Born: June 18, 1963, Leeds, West
　Yorkshire, England.
Height: 5ft 11in.　*Weight:* 12st 0lb.
Position: Centre.
Club: Leeds.
Club Honours
John Player Special Trophy:
　winners 1983/84.

In his first full season in 1983/84,
David showed himself to be an outstanding prospect for the future. He
joined Leeds from Hunslet Parkside
amateurs who, in the previous year,
won all their 24 games. In the final
of the BARLA Youth Cup, David
scored 15 points in his side's 27-2
victory over Cumbrian team Kells.
David a try scoring centre, and
deadly goalkicker, earned Great
Britain honours at Colts level with
Leeds. He was the match winner in
the 1984 John Player Special Trophy with five goals in the final
against Widnes and he kicked two
vital goals in the 12-10 quarter final
replay victory over Bradford Northern in the Challenge Cup.

Jim Crellin
Born: May 19, 1943, Whitehaven,
　Cumbria, England.
Height: 5ft 10in　*Weight:* 13st 7lb.
Position: Coach.
Club: Swinton.
Club Honours

John Player Trophy: runners up
1973/74 (Rochdale), 1976/77
(Blackpool B – coach)
BBC Floodlit Trophy: runners up
1971/72 (Rochdale).

Taking Blackpool Borough to the final of the 1977 John Player Trophy must rank as one of the best coaching feats in modern rugby. The unfashionable seasiders were next to the bottom of the Second Division that season but still Jim managed to steer them all the way to a meeting with powerful Castleford where they lost 25-15.

A former centre or full back, he started his career at Workington before moving to Oldham and then Rochdale. At Rochdale, whom he joined in March 1970, he collected runners up medals in the 1971/72 Floodlit Trophy final, and the 1974 John Player final. After Blackpool, Jim had a spell in charge at Halifax before drifting out of the professional game for a while.

In 1983 he took over at Swinton, following Tommy Grainey, and restored some of the 'Lions' roar as they made a late, but unsuccessful bid for promotion.

Terry Crook

Born: November 27, 1947,
Wakefield, West Yorkshire,
England.
Height: 5ft 11in.   *Weight:* 14st 0lb.
Position: Coach.
Club: Batley.
Club Honours
Yorkshire Cup: runners up 1973/74,
1974/75 (Wakefield Trinity).

Terry took over as coach of the struggling Batley side in the summer of 1982 and, despite finishing third from the bottom of the Second Division that first season, he injected a new enthusiasm into the team. That drive carried on into the next season and while they failed to frighten the big boys, their mid table position was respectable.

As a player Terry started life as second row forward but later moved to centre with his first club, Wakefield. He joined Trinity in 1967 and after ten years moved on to Bramley in 1977 to become joint coach. He returned to Belle Vue two years later as assistant coach and in June 1982 got his first full coaching appointment at Mount Pleasant. He appeared in two losing Yorkshire Cup finals for Trinity. In the 1973 match he kicked Trinity's only two points in the 7-2 defeat by Leeds and in 1974 he kicked two goals as they went down narrowly to Hull KR.

Lee Crooks

Born: September 18, 1963, Hull,
Humberside, England.
Height: 6ft 1in.   *Weight:* 15st 4lb.
Position: Second row forward.
Club: Hull.
Great Britain Honours
Debut (full): October 1982 v
Australia (at Hull City AFC)
(under 24): December 1983 v
France (in Oldham)
Appearances (full): two (one as sub)
(under 24): one.
Club Honours
Division One: winners 1982/83
Challenge Cup: winners 1981/82;
runners up 1982/83
Premiership Trophy: runners up
1981/82, 1982/83
John Player Trophy: winners 1981/
82
Yorkshire Cup: winners 1982/83,
1983/84.

Lee Crooks

Lee played in a local amateur league before signing professional for Hull on his 17th birthday. He was captain of the first Great Britain Colts team to tour Australia and Papua New Guinea in the summer of 1982, and before the end of the year he won his first Great Britain cap as their youngest forward ever. Amazingly, his first – and only, under 24 appearance did not come until December 1983, 12 months after his first full appearance.

Lee was unfortunate not to have won the Man of the Match award in the 1981/82 Premiership final against Widnes, when, despite being on the losing side, he scored one try and kicked two goals and a drop goal. He was equally unfortunate not to win the award in the 1981/82 John Player Trophy final against Hull KR, when he scored eight of his team's 12 points to earn victory over their arch rivals. A painter and decorator by trade, he was selected for the 1984 tour of Australasia.

John Crossley
Born: October 16, 1956, Castleford, West Yorkshire, England.
Height: 5ft 6in. *Weight:* 11st 4lb.
Position: Stand off.
Club: Fulham.
Club Honours
Division Two: winners 1980/81 (York), 1982/83 (Fulham)
Awards: Trumanns Man of Steel Division Two Player of the Year, 1981.

When John crossed the York line to notch his 27th try of 1982/83 he became Fulham's top try scorer in a season. Ironically that try was against his old club, where he is still the top try scorer for a season. He is the *only* current player to hold such an honour with two different clubs simultaneously.

John joined Wakefield Trinity before moving to Wigginton Road, where he helped York win the Second Division in 1980/81, his 34 tries establishing a new divisional record. The following season saw him playing with Fulham, scoring 15 tries. His new club dropped into the Second Division after just one season and it was in the lower division again that John established the London club's try scoring record of 27. That season he also won a Second Division Championship medal as Fulham won the title by three points from Wakefield.

Paul Daley
Born: May 30, 1942, Normanton, West Yorkshire, England.
Height: 5ft 7in. *Weight:* 11st 0lb.
Position: Coach.
Club: Hunslet.
Club Honours
Division Two: winners 1979/80

(Featherstone R – coach)
Yorkshire Cup: winners 1971/72
  (Hull KR)
Championship Play-off: winners
  1964/65 (Halifax).

A top try scoring scrum half in his playing days, Paul's feat of transforming New Hunslet in the mid-seventies far outweighs any success he had as a player. He joined the club as coach in 1975 and turned the Second Division strugglers into a promotion winning side in 1976/77. But the South Leeds club were not fully equipped for the First Division and were relegated again the following season. Paul stood by them during their struggle in the top division but resigned at the start of the 1978/79 season.

He took over at York a couple of months later, and led them to promotion. The following season he was at Featherstone and took them to the First Division at the end of 1979/80 as Second Division champions. Paul re-joined Hunslet in April 1981, and in 1983/84 promotion specialist Paul had them back in the First Division.

Paul's playing career started at Halifax in 1962, following trials at nearby Keighley. He was a member of the Halifax team that won the Championship Play-off in 1965, defeating league champions St. Helens 15-7 in the final. His next port of call was Bradford and then Hull Kingston Rovers. At Craven Park he won his second title in the 1971 Yorkshire Cup as Rovers defeated Castleford 11-7. Paul turned his attention to coaching in 1975.

Andy Dannatt

Born: 1966, Hull, Humberside, England.
Height: 6ft 2in.   *Weight:* 15st 7lb.
Position: Second row forward.
Club: Hull.
Club Honours
Division One: runners up 1983/84
  Colts League: winners 1982/83.

Hailed as one of the discoveries of the 1983/84 season, Andy was selected for the Great Britain training squad for the summer tour of Australia just four days after his debut for Great Britain Colts against France in February. Fast progress considering he had not played his first full game for Hull until January. Andy joined Hull from Villa Youth club in July 1982 and during the following season made only one appearance, as substitute. But he did show promise on the club tour to Australia and New Zealand. Now second row forward, Andy was an all round athlete at Bransholme High School in Hull where he still holds the 800 metres record. Andy works on the groundstaff at The Boulevard.

Tommy David

Born: April 2, 1949, Pontypridd, South Wales.
Height: 6ft 0in.   *Weight:* 15st. 10lb.
Position: Prop.
Club: Cardiff City.
Welsh Honours
Debut: November 1981 v England
  (at Cardiff)
Appearances: two.
Club Honours
Top try scorer: 1982/83 season.

The former Welsh and British Lions back row man joined Cardiff from Pontypridd Rugby Union Side in July 1982 ready for Cardiff's inaugural Rugby League season. He soon settled into the 13 man game and the following season broke several records. He scored 26, a league best for a prop, beating the old record of 25 set the previous season by Carlisle's Mick Morgan. His 26th try – which made him the first front man ever to figure in the top ten try scorers for the season – was scored in the final game of the season against another soccer/rugby league outfit, Fulham. Also in 1982/83, he achieved the rare feat as a prop of scoring four tries, against Swinton in February.

In his RU days Tommy gained four Welsh caps and toured South Africa with the Lions in 1974, although he never played in a Test match. He is a director of his own firm, the appropriately named Triple Crown Industries.

Tommy Dawes

Born: October 11, 1938, Barrow-in-Furness, Cumbria, England.
Height: 5ft 10in. *Weight:* 14st 0lb.
Position: Coach.
Club: Barrow.
Club Honours
Division Two: winners 1983/84 (Barrow – coach)
Lancashire Cup: winners 1983/84 (Barrow – coach)
Awards: Greenalls Man of Steel Coach of the Year 1983/84.

Tommy was born and bred in the shipbuilding town of Barrow so it was certainly a case of local boy makes good as he led the club to the Second Division title in 1984 – breaking all sorts of records in the process – and winning the Lancashire Cup for the first time in 29 years. The County Cup final victory

provided one of the season's biggest upsets as Barrow toppled favourites Widnes 12-8 at Wigan. Tommy took over at Craven Park in May 1983, having been coach at Whitehaven for the previous 12 months, and guided them out of the Second Division.

Full back Tommy joined Barrow from St. Mary's amateur side in January 1958. In more than 300 matches for the club, he kicked over 400 goals and his 102 goals in 1958/59 made him one of only four Barrow players to record more than a century in a season.

Steve Diamond

Born: July 7, 1953, Hereford, England.
Height: 5ft 10in. *Weight:* 12st 6lb.
Position: Centre.
Club: Fulham.
Welsh Honours
Debut: January 1980 v France (in Widnes)
Appearances: two (one as sub).
Club Honours
Second Division: winners 1982/83 (Fulham)
Challenge Cup: runners up 1978/79 (Wakefield Trinity).

Steve joined Fulham at the end of their opening season in the League in readiness to help them in their first season in the top division. But in the event the speedy skills – and goalkicking – of Steve could not save them from relegation. Steve made the switch from Rugby Union in 1978 when he joined Wakefield Trinity from Welsh side Newbridge. He made an immediate impact at Belle Vue, scoring a try on his debut. That early promise did not materialise, although he turned out

Steve Diamond

for Trinity in that year's Cup final at Wembley where they lost 12-3 to a Widnes side captained by his former Fulham coach Reg Bowden. Steve has made three Welsh international appearances and since joining Fulham has twice broken the club goals and points scoring record in a season. He enjoys golf and do-it-yourself.

Kevin Dick

Born: October 27, 1957, Leeds, West Yorkshire, England.
Height: 5ft 7in.   *Weight:* 12st 13lb.
Position: Scrum half.
Club: Leeds.
Great Britain Honours
Debut (full): October 1980 v New Zealand (at Wigan)
Appearances (full): two.
Club Honours
Challenge Cup: winners 1976/77,

1977/78
Premiership Trophy: winners 1978/79
John Player Trophy: winner 1983/84; runners up 1982/83
Yorkshire Cup: winners 1979/80, 1980/81
Man of the Match awards: 1980/81 White Rose Trophy, Yorkshire Cup final, 1978/79 Harry Sunderland Trophy, Premiership final.

Few would have denied Steve Pitchford the Lance Todd award for his non-stop performance for Leeds in the 1977 Challenge Cup final win over Widnes. Equally, there could be little argument as to whom the surprise package of the match was – 19-year-old Kevin Dick. Appearing at scrum half for Leeds in his First Challenge Cup match Kevin's cheeky style of play earned him a try, three goals and a drop. Kevin joined 'The Loiners' from local amateurs, Milford, in 1974, and became an overnight sensation after that Wembley appearance. He returned the following year to pick up a second winners medal to become the youngest person to have won two of them.

In the 1978/79 Premiership final Kevin kicked eight goals in the 24-2 win over Bradford Northern. It was a record for the final which still stands and earned him the Harry Sunderland award, organised by the Rugby League Writer's Association, by an unprecedented unanimous vote. Kevin's goalkicking performances earned him selection for the two Test matches against New Zealand in October/November 1980.

Kevin has appeared in seven major finals for Leeds in seven years, the last being in the 1983/84

Kevin Dick

after he became the club's fourth coach in seven months, Borough called in the Official Receiver. An 11th hour rescue operation by a local hotel chain saved the club and Tommy set about rejuvenating the team. By the end of 1983/84 he had achieved spectacular results, guiding them into the Second Division promotion zone. In his first season in charge Borough ended seven places off the bottom of the Second Division, a minor miracle by their standards.

The magic continued in 1983/84 as Tommy took the side to within a couple of points of promotion to the First Division. Their 20 wins was their most successful League record since they joined in 1954. Tommy is also landlord of the Bowling Green public house adjacent to Wigan's Central Park ground.

John Player Special Trophy final, which gave him his sixth winners medals from those seven appearances. He is a former captain of Great Britain Colts.

Tommy Dickens

Born: November 25, 1943, Wigan,
    Greater Manchester, England.
Height: 5ft 10in.   *Weight:* 13st 10lb.
Position: Coach.
Club: Blackpool Borough.

The job of coach at Blackpool Borough must have been one of the most unenviable positions in Rugby League in March, 1982, but that did not deter Tommy Dickens. Shortly

Colin Dixon

Born: December 3, 1943, Cardiff,
    South Wales.
Height: 5ft 11in.   *Weight:* 15st 6lb.
Position: Coach.
Club: Halifax.
Great Britain Honours
Debut (full): November 1968 v
    France (in St. Helens)
Appearances (full): 12 (two as sub).
Club Honours
Division One: winners 1973/74,
    1975/76 (Salford)
Challenge Cup: runners up 1968/69
    (Salford)
Premiership Trophy: runners up
    1975/76 (Salford)
John Player Trophy: runners up
    1972/73 (Salford)
Championship Play-off: winners
    1964/65 (Halifax); runners up
    1965/66 (Halifax)
Lancashire Cup: winners 1972/73

(Salford); runners up 1973/74, 1974/75, 1975/76 (all Salford)

Yorkshire Cup: winners 1963/64 (Halifax)

BBC Floodlit Trophy: winners 1974/75 (Salford).

Colin's playing career spanned 20 years and more than 700 senior games a total third only in the all time list to Jim Sullivan and Gus Risman. He turned professional with Halifax from Cardiff Juniors in 1961 as a speedy centre, but later moved to the second row. During his spell at Thrum Hall, the club went through its best period since the glory days of the mid-fifties. They won the Yorkshire Cup in 1963 and the following season 1964/65 won the Championship Play-off for the first time since 1907.

Colin moved to Salford for a record £12,000 fee plus a player exchange deal in 1968. He joined a host of other stars at the Willows who started one of the most successful spells in the club's history. At the end of this first full season Colin was in the Challenge Cup final at Wembley where Salford were beaten by Castleford. From 1972/73 until 1975/76 Salford – and Colin – appeared in all the major finals except the Challenge Cup. They won the First Division twice (in 1974 and 1976) and were runners up in the Premiership in the second of those two years. They won the 1974/75 Floodlit Trophy final, defeating Warrington in a replay after a rare 0-0 scoreline in the first game, and appeared in four consecutive Lancashire Cup finals between 1972 and 1975. Their other final appearance was in the John Player Trophy in 1973 but Colin collected a losers' medal despite scoring Salford's try

in the defeat by Leeds.

Colin played for Great Britain in 14 Tests, touring twice – in 1972 for the World Cup and in 1974. He also played in the 1975 World Championship, representing Wales for whom he played ten times. After his glory days at Salford, Dixon moved to Hull KR in September 1980 and part of the legacy he left at Craven Park can be seen in their current success. Having tried a spell of coaching temporarily at Salford in 1976 an 'older and wiser' Colin returned to the job in October 1982 when he took over at his first club, Halifax. But they were relegated at the end of his first season. Undeterred, Colin re- motivated the club and after one season in the Second Division bounced back into the top flight.

Steve Donlan

Born: September 4, 1954, Leigh, Greater Manchester, England.
Height: 5ft 9in.   *Weight:* 12st 7lb.
Position: Centre.
Club: Leigh.
Club Honours
Division One: winners 1981/82
Lancashire Cup: winners 1981/82.

Steve passed 150 consecutive appearances for Leigh last season moving closer to Keith Elwell's all time record. His run started in February 1980 and since then he has scored vital tries for his club, 15 of them coming in their Championship winning season of 1981/82. One of his most dramatic matches was the Lancashire Cup win over Widnes also in 1981/82. With Widnes trailing 5-3, Steve dived on a loose ball over his own goal line. It squirted from his hands for Keith Bentley to touch down. The referee was about to award a try when the touch judge declared Donlan had already made the ball dead. Reprieved, Woods added a penalty for Leigh before Steve added a drop goal for an 8-3 victory. An accountant by profession, Steve was the surprise choice in the Great Britain party for the 1984 tour, having no previous Great Britain experience at any level.

John Dorahy

John Dorahy

Born: 1955, Sydney, Australia.
Height: 5ft 8in.   *Weight:* 12st 0lb.
Position: Centre/stand off.
Club: Hull Kingston Rovers.
Club Honours
Division One: winners 1983/84
Premiership Trophy: winners 1983/84
Man of the Match Awards: Harry Sunderland Trophy – 1984 Premiership final.

John flew in from Australia in October 1983 to join Hull Kingston Rovers from Sydney Premiership side Illawarra. He has re-signed for the 1984/85 season. An Australian Test centre, he proved himself to be a free scoring player as Rovers won the First Division Championship. He also has a liking for scoring goals – he kicked seven of them in one game against Wakefield Trinity, on April Fool's Day.

His first season in England was crowned by his winning the Harry Sunderland Trophy for his outstanding performance as Man of the Match in the Premiership final against Castleford. His one try and one goal, and great all round performance, made him the first overseas winner of the trophy.

Des Drummond

Born: June 17, 1958, Jamaica.
Height: 5ft 8in.   *Weight:* 11st 3lb.
Position: Winger.
Club: Leigh.
Great Britain Honours
Debut (full): November 1980 v New Zealand (in Bradford)
(under 24): November 1979 v France (in Leigh)
Appearances (full): ten
(under 24): five.

Des Drummond

and 1975 and won a bronze medal in the Northern Judo Championships. He is also a fine sprinter as he proved to millions of television viewers during the BBC Superstars Competition. He won the 60 metre and 100 metre sprints – the latter in an impresive time of 10.85 seconds. Britain's Young Player of the Year in 1981 and 1982, Des is Leigh's most capped player ever and added to his total of 10 Great Britain appearances on the 1984 Australasia tour.

An all round sportsman, he also likes to take part in more leisurely activities like snooker and table tennis, and relaxes listening to music.

Club Honours
Division One: winners 1981/82
Lancashire Cup: winners 1981/82
Awards: Trumanns Man of Steel Young Player of the Year – 1981 and 1982.

Jamaican-born Des scored 65 tries for Leigh in the three seasons between 1980/81 and 1982/83. That helped them win the First Division title for only the second time in 1981/82. Des finished joint second in the try scoring list that season with 26.

Des a regular member of the Great Britain squad has made ten international appearances since his debut against New Zealand at Bradford in 1980. A year earlier he had scored on his debut for the under 24 team on his home ground, Hilton Park, against France. Des was North West Judo Champion in 1974

Ronnie Duane
Born: May 31, 1963, Warrington, Cheshire, England.
Height: 6ft 1in.   *Weight:* 13st 10lb.
Position: Centre.
Club: Warrington.
Great Britain Honours
Debut (full): February 1983 v France (in Carcassonne) (under 24): January 1983 v France (in Carpentras)
Appearances (full): three (under 24): two.
Club Honours
Lancashire Cup: winners 1982/83.

Ronnie's versatility was never more evident than on the Great Britain Colts tour of 1982. Struck down by injuries, the side was deprived of four of its top forwards. But Ronnie stepped into the breach, moving from his normal centre position into the pack and gave another of his dynamic performances.

An amateur with the local Woolston side, he signed for Warrington in April 1981. His early career was

Ronnie Duane

side for the first time in 1984, Ronnie was injured after only ten minutes of the tourists' opening game and played no further part in the tour. The future looks good for Ronnie and it should not be long before he is adding to his collection of club honours, which presently stand at one Lancashire Cup winners medal. His brother Ian also plays for Warrington.

Shaun Dunford

Born: 1961, Dewsbury, West
  Yorkshire, England.
Height: 5ft 6in.   *Weight:* 11st 7lb.
Position: Winger.
Club: Dewsbury.
Club Honours
Leading goal kicker: 1980/81, 1981/
  82, 1982/83, 1983/84.

Shaun has been Dewsbury's leading scorer for the past four seasons, amassing more than 500 points. The 1983/84 season was one of his best kicking over 75 goals and scoring in 31 consecutive matches.
  Shaun kicked nine goals against Workington Town in April 1982, one short of the club record.

Brian Dunn

Born: March 16, 1963, St. Helens,
  Merseyside, England.
Height: 6ft 2in.   *Weight:* 14st 7lb.
Position: Second row.
Club: Wigan.
Great Britain Honours
Debut (under 24): November 1983 v
  France (in Villeneuve)
  Appearances
  (under 24): two

A joiner by trade, Brian went to Wigan from Pilkington Recs in Jan-

dogged with injury, but his first full season – 1982/83 – saw him display some amazing talents. One of his best performances that season was in the John Player Trophy semi-final game with Wigan. Although ending up on the losing side, he scored two of his side's four tries – both of outstanding quality. His performance in that match led to his selection for the under 24 team against France later that same month, and the following month he was back in France, with the senior Great Britain squad.
  Touring with the Great Britain

uary, 1982, but had to wait until the following season before making his senior debut. He played 11 games, and would have appeared in more during the 1983/84 season but for a transfer request. He was listed at £45,000, a price tag that discouraged potential buyers St. Helens.

He was chosen for the Great Britain under 24 side in the two matches with France in November/December 1983. The day his selection was announced (after he had played 20 senior games) he was appealing against a two match suspension. Fortunately for Brian he was successful; if his appeal had failed he would have missed the first of the internationals.

Bob Eccles

Born: July 10, 1957, St. Helens,
Merseyside, England.
Height: 6ft 1in. *Weight:* 15st 4lb.
Position: Second row forward.
Club: Warrington.
Great Britain Honours
Debut (full): November 1982 v
Australia (in Wigan)
(under 24): October 1978 v
Australia (in Hull)
Appearances (full): one
(under 24): two.
Club Honours
John Player Trophy: winners 1980/
81
Lancashire Cup: winners 1980/81,
1982/83.

Discovered by coach Alex Murphy playing local amateur soccer five years ago, Bob revealed his full potential during the 1982/83 season. Records galore fell the way of this tough forward, his 22 tries in the First Division were a divisional

Bob Eccles

record by a forward, beating the old record of 19 held by David Hobbs. And his total of 37 in all matches made him the leading try scorer – only the second time a forward had taken that title. In addition, he equalled the John Player Trophy record with five tries in the match with Blackpool Borough in December, and in one spell scored 13 touchdowns in 14 games – nine of them consecutive.

He was called into the Great Britain squad for the first Test against the 1982 Kangaroos as 17th man. He made his debut in the second Test at Wigan, but was on the wrong end of a 27-6 drubbing. Employed by a local brewery, Bob played with Rochdale Colts between November 1976 and March 1977 before being signed by Warrington. He was playing substitute in the 1978/79 John Player final defeat by Widnes, but was in the team two years later when they beat Barrow to win the trophy for a record third time.

David Eckersley

Born: October 10, 1948, Leigh,
    Greater Manchester, England.
Height: 5ft 9in.   *Weight:* 12st 0lb.
Position: Utility back.
Club: Fulham.
Great Britain Honours
Debut (full): November 1973 v
    Australia (in Leeds)
Appearances (full): two (two as
    sub).
Club Honours
First Division: winners 1974/75 (St.
    Helens), 1977/78 (Widnes)
Second Division: winners 1982/83
    (Fulham)
Challenge Cup: winners 1970/71
    (Leigh), 1978/79 (Widnes);
    runners up 1975/76, 1976/77 (both
    Widnes)
Premiership Trophy: winners 1979/
    80 (Widnes); runners up 1977/78
    (Widnes)
John Player Trophy: winners 1978/
    79 (Widnes) runners up 1977/78,
    1979/80 (both Widnes)
Lancashire Cup: winners 1970/71
    (Leigh), 1976/77, 1978/79, 1979/80
    (all Widnes); runners up 1969/70
    (Leigh)
Man of the Match awards:
    1978/79 John Player trophy final;
    1976/77 Lancashire Cup final.

When Reggie Bowden took David Eckersley to Fulham from Widnes with him in 1980, he knew he was

taking a man with a wealth of talent and experience. Reg and David had played together in 11 major Cup finals and had ended up on the winning side in six of them. Eckersley joined his home town Club, Leigh, from their Colts team in January 1968, and in 1971 enjoyed one of the greatest moments of his career, when he helped them win the Challenge Cup final at Wembley with a try and a drop goal.

Shortly afterwards David moved a few miles down the East Lancashire Road to join St. Helens, in September 1972. After the 'Saints' won the First Division title in 1974/75, David moved on to Widnes. At Naughton Park he shared the great revival to appear in those 11 senior finals for the Cheshire side.

He turned in one of his finest displays during the 1978/79 John Player final at St. Helens to win the Man of the Match award. David played for Great Britain four times

David Eckersley

while with St. Helens, ironically the period of his career in which he enjoyed the least success club-wise. He made his debut as substitute against Australia at Leeds in November 1973. Now nearing the end of a fine career, David spends his relaxation hours either listening to popular music, swimming, playing tennis – or watching soccer.

Shaun Edwards

Born: October 17, 1966, Wigan
    Greater Manchester, England.
Height: 5ft 9in.   *Weight:* 11st 12lb.
Position: Scrum half/stand off/
    winger.
Club: Wigan.
Club Honours
Challenge Cup: runners up 1983/84.

Every sport has its golden boys and Wigan's Shaun Edwards is the latest to hit Rugby League. A versatile back, he joined Wigan amid the kind of razzmatazz normally afforded to show business personalities. The £35,000 signing on his 17th birthday was completed in front of the television cameras. Shaun, captain of England schoolboys at both league and union, is the son of Jackie Edwards, former Warrington and Great Britain player.

He had half a dozen clubs vying for his signature before Wigan clinched the deal. He was thrown into the first team immediately because of an injury crisis and made his debut in the John Player Special Trophy match with York in November 1983. He was selected by Great Britain Colts for their two matches with the French in 1984, but had to withdraw through injury. But a couple of months later he was at Wembley as Wigan met Widnes in the Challenge Cup final. He was the youngest player to appear in the final. He spent most of his first season on the wing learning his trade and keen to improve.

He hoped to be spending the summer of 1984 playing with Balmain in Australia, but his father felt he was too young to be playing in that standard of rugby – instead he toured with the British Universities and Colleges side.

Mark Elia

Born: December 25, 1962,
    Auckland, New Zealand.
Height: 6ft 0in.   *Weight:* 13st 7lb.
Position: Winger/centre.
Club: Kent Invicta.
Club Honours
Leading try scorer: 1983/84.

A former premier grade player with New Zealand side Te Atatu, Mark came over to England with the intention of playing cricket with Surrey, but ended up playing Rugby League for Kent Invicta. He joined Kent at the start of their League campaign and, in crossing the Batley line three times during a Championship match in February, 1984, became the first Kent player to score a hat trick of tries. An all-round sportsman, he has run the 100 metres in 10.35 seconds – only 1/10th of a second ouside Allan Wells' winning time at the Moscow Olympics.

Keith Elwell

Born: February 12, 1950, Widnes,
    Cheshire, England.
Height: 5ft 7in.   *Weight:* 12st 7lb.
Position: Hooker.

Club: Widnes.
Great Britain Honours
Debut (full): June 1977 v Australia
    (in Sydney – World Cup)
Appearances (full): three.
Club Honours
Division One: winners 1977/78
Challenge Cup: winners 1974/75,
    1978/79, 1980/81, 1983/84;
    runners up 1975/76, 1976/77,
    1981/82
Premiership Trophy: winners 1979/
    80, 1981/82, 1982/83; runners up
    1977/78
John Player Trophy: winners 1975/
    76, 1978/79; runners up 1974/75,
    1977/78, 1979/80, 1983/84
Lancashire Cup: winners 1974/75,
    1975/76, 1976/77, 1978/79, 1979/
    80; runners up 1981/82, 1983/84
BBC Floodlit Trophy: winners 1978/
    79; runners up 1972/73, 1973/74.

The 1984 Challenge Cup final was
the 27th major final Widnes had
appeared in since the 1972/73
season, and hooker Keith Elwell has
played in every one. This unprecedented run started with a
defeat by Leigh in the 1972/73
Floodlit final, Keith has appeared in
at least one final every year since.
His most successful season came in
1978/79 when he appeared in four
finals, and won all of them,
Challenge Cup, John Player Trophy, Lancashire Cup, and Floodlit
Trophy.
    At that time, Keith was in the
middle of an amazing sequence of
consecutive appearances for the
club. Starting with the 1977
Challenge Cup final against Leeds
and ending with the game against
St Helens on September 5, 1982,
Keith played 239 games in a row –
beating Gilbert Austin's 60-year-old
record. He even withdrew from the

England team to play France in
1981 to make the record possible.
When he appeared in the 1984
Challenge Cup final he became one
of only three men to have been in
seven Wembley Cup finals. Team
mates Mick Adams and Eric Hughes
are the others.
    Keith's introduction to the sport
came at St. Michael's Junior School
– the same school attended by Mick
Adams. But it was at cricket that
Keith gained his first representative honours – for Widnes schoolboys. Keith was a member of the
England 'shadow squad' for the 1975
World Championship but did not
make his England debut until 1978.
The previous year he toured Australia with Great Britain and
gained his first cap in the World
Cup *final* at Sydney.
    Considering his record at club
level, it is surprising Keith only has
three Great Britain and two
England appearances to his credit.
Employed as a chemical operator,
Keith relaxes by listening to music
and reading. His loyalty to the
Naughton Park club was rewarded
with a bumper £30,000 benefit in
the 1980/81 season.

Keith England

Born: February 27, 1964,
    Castleford, West Yorkshire,
    England.
Height: 5ft 8in.   *Weight:* 14st 1lb.
Position: Loose forward.
Club: Castleford.
Great Britain Honours
Debut (under 24): November 1983 v
    France (in Villeneuve)
Appearances (under 24): one as sub.
Club Honours
Yorkshire Cup: runners up 1983/84.

Loose forward Keith has a reputation as an attacking player and that gained him selection as a substitute for the Great Britain under 24 side against France at Villeneuve in November 1983. He came on after half an hour for Hull's Wayne Proctor.

Keith toured Papua New Guinea and Australia, with Great Britain Colts in 1982, playing in six matches and scoring one try. On his return he became a regular member of the Castleford senior squad, having helped Castleford to third place in the Colts league behind the two Hull giants.

Steve Evans

Born: June 6, 1958, Featherstone, West Yorkshire, England.
Height: 6ft 1in.   *Weight:* 13st 5lb.
Position: Stand off/centre.
Club: Hull, Featherstone Rovers.
Great Britain Honours
Debut (full): June 1979 v Australia (in Brisbane)
(under 24): November 1980 v New Zealand (in Fulham)
Appearances (full): seven (three as sub)
(under 24): three.
Club Honours
Division One: winners 1982/83 (Hull)
Division Two: winners 1979/80 (Featherstone Rovers)
Challenge Cup: winners 1981/82 (Hull); runners up 1982/83 (Hull)
Premiership Trophy: runners up 1981/82, 1982/83 (both Hull)
Yorkshire Cup: winners 1977/78 (Featherstone Rovers) winners 1982/83 (Hull)
Awards: Trumanns Man of Steel Young Player of the Year for 1979.

Steve Evans

Who is the only player to have appeared for two different teams in the Challenge Cup in one season? Answer – Steve Evans in 1981/82. Steve turned out for Featherstone Rovers in a qualifying match in the 1981/82 competition. He joined Hull in February and, without infringing the rules, went all the way to Wembley. No other player will emulate the feat, as the rules have now been changed.

Steve has another record. He was the only Great Britain player to score a try against the invincible Australians in 1982. He has a reputation as a good captain and led the under 24 team in all three matches he played for them. His early Rugby days were spent with Normanton RUFC. From there he joined Featherstone, playing with their Supporters, under 17's and under 18's sides, before making the senior team in 1976. That same year he captained the Great Britain under 18 team against France. He toured Australasia with Great Britain in 1979 and was leading tryscorer with 16.

A £70,000 cheque took him to the progressive Hull outfit in February 1982, making him the second most expensive player in the game's history. In the final League game of the 1983/84 season, the first of his two tries for Hull gave him a career total of 100 League tries, the youngest player to reach the milestone.

He spent most of his early career commuting between Walsall in the West Midlands and Featherstone as he was a student teacher in Walsall. However, he now earns his living as an insurance agent, and being an all round athlete, enjoys squash, badminton, canoeing and athletics.

George Fairbairn

Born: July 25, 1954, Peebles, Scotland.
Height: 5ft 11in.   *Weight:* 12st 10lb.
Position: Full back.
Club: Hull Kingston Rovers.
Great Britain Honours
Debut (full): June 1977 v France (in Auckland – World Cup)
Appearances (full): 17.
Club Honours
Division One: winners 1983/84
Premiership Trophy: winners 1983/84
John Player Trophy: runners up 1981/82 (Hull KR)
Lancashire Cup: runners up 1980/81 (Wigan)
Awards: Trumanns Man of Steel – 1980.

When George moved across the Pennines from Wigan to Hull Kingston

Rovers in June 1981 he became, at £72,000, Rugby League's most expensive player. His move caused a sensation as the fee nearly doubled the previous record of £40,000 paid a year earlier by Hull when buying Trevor Skerrett from Wakefield. George had been player/coach at Wigan and was released by them shortly after taking them to the First Division.

George made a sensational start with Hull KR breaking Neil Fox's club record for the most number of goals in one season by 20 with 166. Also in that first season he became the third player behind Steve Hesford and Sammy Lloyd to kick 500 goals and score 1000 First Division points since the re-introduction of the Division system in 1973/74. Fairbairn joined Wigan from Scottish Rugby Union club Kelso in 1974. Although Scottish he was picked for the England squad for the 1975 World Championships – after only half a season in Rugby League. He played in seven of England's eight World Championship matches – kicking 26 goals and scoring two tries. George made his Great Britain debut in the opening World Cup game with France at Auckland in 1977 and celebrated with seven goals. In his first six Test match appearances he scored a total of 26 goals.

Surprisingly, he was left out of the squad for the 1979 tour, but was flown out as replacement for the injured Tommy Martyn of Warrington and played in the last three Tests against Australia and both matches against New Zealand. Considering George's goalkicking records and international career it is amazing that until 1984 all the major honours have eluded him at club level. Prior to winning Division One and the Premiership in 1984 he had only two runners up medals. The first with Wigan in the Lancashire Cup in 1980/81 and the second with Hull KR in the John Player Trophy the following year. However, his skills were duly recognised when he won the Trumanns Man of Steel award for 1980. George plays squash and golf and enjoys gardening.

George Fairbairn

Frank Feighan
Born: February 28, 1957, London, England.
Height: 5ft 11in.   *Weight:* 13st 8lb.
Position: Winger.
Club: Kent Invicta.

Frank joined League newcomers Kent Invicta in July 1983 from London based amateur Rugby League side Peckham. But he had played one League game for Fulham earlier in the 1982/83 season, scoring a try against Blackpool. Frank scored two tries in front of the television cameras as Kent lost to Castleford in the Challenge Cup in 1984. His elusive style of play was typified by one fine score which Alex Murphy described as the 'try of the season'.

Steve Fenwick
Born: July 23, 1951, Caerphilly, Wales.
Height: 5ft 10in.   *Weight:* 13st 6lb.
Position: Centre.
Club: Cardiff City.
Welsh Honours
Debut: November 1981 v England (in Cardiff)
Appearances: two.
Club Honours
Top points scorer: 1981/82, 1982/83, 1983/84.

Cardiff paid £20,000 to bring Steve from Bridgend rugby union club in August 1981, their highest ever fee. The crash-tackling former Welsh Rugby Union captain Has been the club's leading points scorer in each of their three seasons in the League. And in 1982/83 he kicked a record 110 goals for the club, beating his 108 kicked the previous season. In the game against Swinton on February 20, 1983 he kicked a club record eight goals.

Steve played 30 times for Wales RU team between 1975 and 1981 and four times for the British Lions during their 1977 tour of New Zealand. Since joining the professional game, Steve has appeared in both internationals played by Wales against England and Australia and kicked five goals in those two games.

Steve Ferres

Born: December 17, 1953,
   Castleford, West Yorkshire,
   England.
Height: 5ft 9in.   *Weight:* 12st 10lb.
Position: Stand off.
Club: Carlisle.
Club Honours
Division One: winners 1979/80,
   1980/81 (Bradford N)
Premiership Trophy: runners up
   1978/79, 1979/80 (Bradford
   Northern)
John Player Trophy: winners 1979/
   80 (Bradford N).

Steve's 111 goals helped Carlisle to promotion after their first season in the League in 1983. They put him just five short of a top ten placing – which would have been his first during his lengthy career. He began at Bramley and stayed in Yorkshire, first with York, then Dewsbury, and on to Bradford Northern. The deal that took him to Odsal saw Bob Haigh go the other way in an exchange in 1976.

Initially only a reserve at Bradford, he got his big chance when Nigel Stephenson was injured. From that day he maintained a fairly regular first team position. He won *all* his honours with Northern: a John Player Trophy winners medal in 1979/80, two Division One championship medals and two Premiership finals.

Steve joined Carlisle in May 1981 in a £12,000 transfer which also took Bradford colleague Jimmy Thompson to Cumbria. Steve had loan spells with Keighley and Kent Invicta during the 1983/84 season.

John Fieldhouse

Born: June 28, 1962, Wigan,

Greater Manchester, England.
Height: 6ft 0in.   *Weight:* 14st 7lb.
Position: Second row forward.
Club: Warrington.
Great Britain Honours
Debut (under 24): January 1983 v
   France (in Carpentras)
Appearances (under 24): one (one as
   sub).
Club Honours
Lancashire Cup: winners 1982/83.

John joined Warrington from the crack Wigan junior side, St. Patricks, in 1980. He played five games for Warrington during the 1980/81 season, when they finished runners up to Bradford Northern in the first division, and the following season earned himself a regular position in the club's second row.

Try scoring has long been his outstanding talent. He once scored a record six in an under 16 game, against Castleford. He continued to demonstrate the knack at international level, scoring on his under 24 debut in January 1983. He was listed at a world record £82,500 during the 1983/84 season. Widnes showed an interest, but were frightened off by the price tag and John was subsequently withdrawn from sale.

John was the first winner of the Boy of the Year award in the National Coaching scheme held at Butlins, Filey, in the late seventies. A joiner by trade, he enjoys coaching youngsters himself.

Eric Fitzsimmons

Born: October 23, 1948, Oldham,
   Greater Manchester, England.
Height: 5ft 9in.   *Weight:* 12st 0lb.
Position: Winger.
Club: Hunslet.

Club Honours
Runner up as League leading
  goalscorer 1982/83 season.

On 15th September 1982, Hunslet's
Eric Fitzsimmons kicked four goals
against Wakefield Trinity. He went
on to score in the club's next 58
matches with the sequence ending
only when he broke a leg in the
game with Rochdale Hornets on
March 4, 1984. By then his run of 58
consecutive scoring matches placed
him fifth on the all-time list and five
short of the club record.

Eric who cost only £2,000 from
Oldham in August 1981 was Hunslet's top points scorer in his first
season and the following year was
just 15 goals behind the League's
top kicker, Steve Diamond. He holds
the Hunslet record for the most
goals in a season, since the re-
formation of the club in 1973.

Eric played one match as an
amateur for soccer club Bradford
Park Avenue, their penultimate
game in the Football League,
against Chesterfield in April 1970.
He left Rugby League in December
1980 to play local soccer again, but
returned after only two months.

Terry Flanagan

Born: November 27, 1960, Oldham,
  Greater Manchester, England.
Height: 6ft 0in.   *Weight:* 13st 7lb.
Position: Loose forward.
Club: Oldham.
Great Britain Honours
Debut (full): February 1983 v
  France (in Carcassonne)
  (under 24): November 1980 v New
  Zealand (in Fulham)
Appearances (full): two
  (under 24): five.
Club Honours

Division Two: winners 1981/82.

Terry, a Bachelor of Science in elec-
tronic engineering at Manchester
University joined Oldham from
local top amateur side Saddleworth
Rangers in 1979.

He had played for Lancashire at
Schoolboy and Colts level before
joining Oldham and has since
played for them at senior level. He
was appointed club captain at the
age of 19 and led the side to the
Second Division title two years
later.

He was made captain of the Great
Britain under 24 side for the match
against France in November 1983,
replacing Bradford's Brian Noble
who was injured. His brother Kevin
was a skilled forward with Rochdale
Hornets, and Oldham. Terry was
called in as a late replacement (for
Chris Arkwright, who injured his
knee) for the 1984 tour.

Geoff Fletcher

Born: December 10, 1944, St.
  Helens, Merseyside, England.
Height: 6ft 2in.   *Weight:* 16st 10lb.
Position: Player/coach.
Club: Runcorn Highfield.
Club Honours
Championship Play-off: runners up
  1970/71 (Wigan)
Lancashire Cup: winners 1971/72
  (Wigan); runners up 1966/67,
  1968/69 (both Oldham)
BBC Floodlit final: winners 1972/73
  (Leigh); runners up 1976/77
  (Leigh)

One of the game's greatest charac-
ters, Geoff has been coach of struggling Runcorn (previously known as
Huyton) for seven years, making
him one of the longest serving coa-

Terry Flanagan

ches. He saw service with Leigh (twice), Oldham and Wigan before joining Huyton in August 1977 as coach.

A fine, distributing prop forward his qualities were obvious in the 1972/73 Floodlit Trophy final as he helped Leigh beat Widnes. The previous season he had been a member of the Wigan team which defeated the 'Chemics' in the final of the Lancashire Cup. He made a playing comeback at Huyton in 1984, showing he had lost little of his skills and his return coincided with the club's successful run at the end of the season.

Geoff, a St. Helens-based farmer, has been recognised for his devotion to the game with a succession of individual awards, including the inaugural Rugby League Writer's Association Special Award of Merit in 1981.

Phil Ford

Born: March 16, 1961, Cardiff, Wales.
Height: 5ft 11in.　*Weight:* 12st 7lb.
Position: Winger.
Club: Warrington.
Great Britain Honours
Debut (under 24): February 1982 v France (in Tonneins)
Appearances (under 24): one.
Club Honours
Division One: runners up 1980/81.

Welsh winger Phil Ford joined Warrington from Cardiff RUFC in January 1981. He played only five matches that first season, but scored four vital tries as the Wire almost clinched the First Division title finishing just two points behind winners Bradford.

He gained his only international honour when playing for the Great Britain under 24 side against France at Tonneins in February 1982. Later that year he scored a hat trick of tries in the opening Lancashire Cup round against Huyton. Warrington went on to lift the Trophy.

Frank Foster

Born: April 25, 1940, Maryport, Cumbria, England.
Height: 6ft 0in.   *Weight:* 16st 0lb.
Position: Coach.
Club: Whitehaven.
Great Britain Honours
Debut (full): November 1967 v Australia (at White City, London)
Appearances (full): one.
Club Honours
Division Two: winner 1975/76 (Barrow – coach)
John Player Trophy: runners up 1980/81 (Barrow – coach)
Yorkshire Cup: winners 1966/67, 1967/68 (Hull KR)
Championship Play-off: runners up 1967/68 (Hull KR).

Frank, one of the longest serving coaches in the game, left Barrow after ten years in 1983 to take over at nearby Whitehaven. The club had just been promoted to the First Division and Frank and his team struggled in the first half of the season, suffering heavy defeats. But by the end they went down in style, putting up several fine performances against the top teams.

Foster has now accumulated so much young talent around him that Whitehaven are being tipped as the team to take the Second Division by storm in the 1984/85 season. As a player, Frank was a tough, uncompromising loose forward or second rower. During his stay at Hull KR he won two Yorkshire Cup winners medals and was on the losing side in the 1968 Championship Play-off.

He also gained his only international honour in the 1967 second Test against Australia. The game was played at White City, London – the first time Britain had played an international in the Capital since 1908.

Kenny Foulkes

Born: January 27, 1944, Castleford, West Yorkshire, England.
Height: 5ft 4in.   *Weight:* 10st 8lb.
Position: Assistant coach.
Club: Hull.
Club Honours
Division Two: winners 1976/77 (Hull)
John Player Trophy: runners up 1975/76 (Hull).

Kenny was assistant coach to Arthur Bunting at Hull and took over the reins for six weeks during 1983/84 when Bunting took time off due to ill health. Kenny started his career at Castleford and moved to Hull in 1966. He crowned his benefit season of 1976 with a John Player Trophy final against Widnes. Hull, a Second Division side at the time, put up a tremendous performance before narrowly losing 19-13 to the cup favourites.

Deryck Fox

Born: September 17, 1964,
Dewsbury, West Yorkshire,
England.
Height: 5ft 6in.   *Weight:* 11st 0lb.
Position: Scrum half.
Club: Featherstone Rovers.
Club Honours
Players' Union Player of the Year,
1983/84.

Deryck, a former BARLA Youth International, had attracted the interest of several pro clubs before he joined Featherstone Rovers from Dewsbury amateur side St. John Fisher in 1983.

His first season at Post Office Road was crowned with a magnificent performance in the Championship match with Whitehaven on November 13, when he scored 24 points, two tries and eight goals, five short of Steve Quinn's Club record. The season ended with Deryck winning the club's Player of the Season and Most Promising Newcomer awards. He also lifted the Players' Union Player of the Year award.

Peter Fox

Born: 1936, Sharlston, Near
Featherstone, West Yorkshire,
England.
Height: 5ft 10in.   *Weight:* 14st 0lb.
Position: Coach.
Club: Bradford Northern.
Club Honours
Division One: winners 1979/80,
1980/81 (Bradford N – coach)
Challenge Cup: winners 1972/73
(Featherstone – coach); runners
up 1973/74 (Featherstone – coach)
Premiership Trophy: winners 1977/
78 (Bradford N – coach); runners
up 1978/79, 1979/80 (Bradford N –
coach)
John Player Trophy: winners 1979/
80 (Bradford N – coach)
Yorkshire Cup: winners 1978/79
(Bradford N – coach); runners up
1981/82, 1982/83 (Bradford N –
coach)
Awards: Trumanns Man of Steel
Coach of the Year – 1980.

One of the most successful present day coaches in the game, Peter Fox claims much of his success stems from the many years he spent playing with struggling Batley. The experience of appearing on so many losing sides taught Peter how to motivate players.

His first coaching appointment was with a local pub side in the Wakefield area. But it was at nearby Featherstone that he enjoyed his first success, a Challenge Cup win in 1973 over the club he now coaches, Bradford Northern. He took the tiny Yorkshire mining town back to Wembley again the following year, but this time to taste defeat at the hands of Warrington. Peter became coach at Bradford in April 1977 after spells at Wakefield and Bramley, and has led them to victory in every major competition – except the Challenge Cup – and his skills earned him the Trumanns Coach of the Year for 1980.

Coach of the Great Britain side that went down 2-1 in the Test series with Australia in Britain in 1978, Peter remains bitter at being replaced as coach for the tour Down under the following summer. He points out he was the last coach not to be 'whitewashed' by the Aussies. The older brother of Don and Neil, he never experienced the same playing success as them. But his record as a coach is outstanding.

Des Foy

Des Foy

Born: December 29, 1963, Oldham,
Greater Manchester, England.
Height: 5ft 11in.   *Weight:* 13st 1lb.
Position: Stand off.
Club: Oldham.
Great Britain Honours
Debut (full): January 1984 v France
(in Avignon)
(under 24): November 1983 v
France (in Villeneuve)
Appearances (full): one
(under 24): two.

Des played for Lancashire and England schoolboys before being snapped up by Widnes for a then record £17,000 contract from amateur side Saddleworth Rangers in July 1980. However, he never quite fitted into the Widnes team, making only 18 first team appearances for them and

scoring seven tries. A permanent move to Oldham followed a spell on loan in January 1983 and since then Des has enjoyed a considerable upsurge in his career. Brian Hogan went the other way as part of the deal.

Des was selected for the Great Britain under 24 team for the match with France at Villeneuve the next November and then in January 1984 he turned out for the full Great Britain team in the first Test with the French at Avignon. He was also selected for the 1984 tour of Australia. His brother Martin is a stand off with Wigan, and his father Derek is on the coaching team at Oldham.

Clayton Friend

Born: March 22, 1962, Auckland,
New Zealand.
Height: 5ft 6in.   *Weight:* 12st 0lb.
Position: Scrum half.
Club: Carlisle.
New Zealand Honours
Debut (full): 1982 v Australia
Appearances (full): two.

One of three New Zealanders recruited by Carlisle for the start of their first season in the top division in 1982/83, Clayton could not help the club from avoiding the drop back down. He gave some fine performances at scrum half and, after touring Britain with the Maoris in October/November 1983 was invited to rejoin the Cumbrian side.

Clayton plays for Manukau back home, and has also represented Auckland in inter-state matches.

Brian Gartland

Born: February 22, 1936, St.

Helens, Merseyside, England.
Height: 5ft 9in.   *Weight:* 12st 7lb.
Position: Coach.
Club: Oldham.

Born in St. Helens, Brian has spent most of his coaching career in the Oldham area. He had enjoyed success with Oldham Colts and 'A' team when Oldham were hit by the resignation of two coaches in quick succession. Brian was asked if he wanted the job in a temporary capacity and stepped in mid way through the 1983/84 season.

Considering the difficulties the club were enduring at the time he did a fine job. Not only did he consolidate First Division status, he also pushed the club to within a touch of a Premiership place.

Carl Gibson

Born: April 23, 1963, Batley, West
  Yorkshire, England.
Height: 5ft 9in   *Weight* 11st 10lb.
Position: Winger.
Club: Batley.
Club Honours
Top try scorer 1982/83, 1983/84
Player of the Year (Club) 1982/83.

A product of the local Batley Boys Amateur Rugby League side, Carl joined Batley in July 1981. He made only three first team appearances in that first season and scored his first senior try in the Second Division game with Keighley in the April. The next season, however, saw him hold down a regular place on the wing. He was the club's top try scorer with 15 and voted the club's Player of the Year. He was top scorer again in 1983/84.

Carl's greatest asset is his speed — he was a former schools 440 yards

and 880 yards champion. But he is also a fearsome tackler and has attracted the attention of several larger clubs. He has so far resisted a move because he prefers to play on with a group of colleagues who signed professional at the same time.

Henderson Gill

Born: January 16, 1961,
  Huddersfield, West Yorkshire,
  England.
Height: 5ft 7in.   *Weight:* 12st 6lb.
Position: Winger.
Club: Wigan.
Great Britain Honours
Debut (full): December 1981 v
  France (in Hull)
  (under 24): January 1982 v
  France (in Leeds)
Appearances (full): three
  (under 24): one.
Club Honours
Challenge Cup: runners up 1983/84
  (Wigan)
John Player Trophy: winners 1982/
  83 (Wigan).

Unpredictable, talented and temperamental, are all labels given to this powerfully built black wingman. Born in Huddersfield, he began his professional career with Bradford Northern. He could not settle at Odsal and just before the start of the 1980/81 season they sold him to Rochdale Hornets for £10,000. The move to Rochdale worked wonders. In October 1981, Wigan paid £30,000 for him and two months later he was making his debut for the full Great Britain side. That game against the French at Hull is one Henderson will never forget. The wing pair of himself and Des Drummond ran in a record five

Who's Who in Rugby League

Henderson Gill

tries and Gill's hat trick was the first by a Great Britain player since Keith Fielding in 1974. It was also the first hat trick on home soil by a British player since Bill Burgess scored three against France at St. Helens in 1968.

Henderson's game has improved considerably since the move to Wigan, and he was a member of the 1983 winning John Player Trophy team, scoring one of his team's tries, before going off with a shoulder injury.

Peter Glynn

Born: January 7, 1954, Widnes, Cheshire, England.
Height: 5ft 11in.   *Weight:* 12st 3lb.
Position: Stand off.
Club: Salford.
England Honours
Debut: March 1979 v Wales (in Widnes)
Appearances: two.
Club Honours
Division One: winners 1974/75 (St. Helens)
Challenge Cup: winners 1975/76 (St. Helens); runners up 1977/78 (St. Helens)
Premiership Trophy: winners 1975/76, 1976/77 (St. Helens)
BBC2 Floodlit Trophy: runners up 1977/78, 1978/79 (St. Helens)

Peter became Rugby League's supersub in the 1976 Challenge Cup final. Only on the bench as a late inclusion he replaced the injured Bill Benyon and in an amazing last six minutes scored two tries to give St. Helens a 20-5 victory. Peter, who joined St. Helens from amateur rugby in the Widnes area, made a second-losing-Wembley appearance two years later. In 1978 he scored

five tries in the match against Hull, one short of the club record. He made two England appearances in 1979 and was selected for the Great Britain tour later in that year. After almost ten years' service at Knowsley Road, Peter moved to Salford in a player exchange deal with Steve Rule in 1983.

Andy Goodway

Born: June 2, 1961, Castleford, West Yorkshire, England.
Height: 6ft 0in.   *Weight:* 15st 0lb.
Position: Second row forward.
Club: Oldham.
Great Britain Honours
Debut (full): February 1983 v France (in Carcassonne)
(under 24): January 1983 v France (in Carpentras)
Appearances (full): three (under 24): two.
Club Honours
Division Two: winners 1981/82.

Andy was sent off three times in the 1983/84 season. But his competitive instincts are matched by his outstanding skills. He joined Oldham from local Featherstone amateur side, Redhill, in 1978. His honours have been scarce at club level – just a Second Division championship medal- but internationally he has made five full and under 24 Great Britain appearances.

He made his debut for the under 24 team against France at Carpentras in January 1983 and a month later, was scoring a try on his debut for the full Test side, also against France in Carcassonne. His performances earned him selection for the 1984 tour of Australia. Andy – a milkman – is a fitness fanatic and enjoys all sports training.

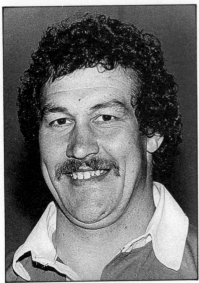
Jeff Grayshon

1975/76 (Dewsbury).

A product of Batley High School, Jeff joined local amateur side, Dawson Brothers.

He was spotted by Dewsbury and signed in 1969. Dewsbury switched him from full back to second row and he was in the pack when the club sprang a surprise by winning the Championship Play-off final in 1973, defeating Leeds 22-13. Jeff appeared for England in the 1975 World Cup, but collected a knee ligament injury which seemed to have ended his career.

He took up coaching at Dewsbury, but was tempted to start playing again. Eventually he performed so well that Bradford Northern came in with a bid and he signed on October 3, 1978.

Soon after joining Northern he regained his England place and in June the following year made his Great Britain debut on the Australian tour.

Jeff's 16-year-old son Paul joined Bradford in 1984.

Jeff Grayshon

Born: March 4, 1949, Birstall, Batley, West Yorkshire, England.
Height: 6ft 2in.   *Weight:* 15st 12lb.
Position: Second row.
Club: Bradford Northern.
Great Britain Honours
Debut (full): June 1979 v Australia (in Sydney)
Appearances (full): 11.
Club Honours
First Division: winners 1979/80, 1980/81 (Bradford N)
Championship Play-off: winners 1972/73 (Dewsbury)
Premiership Trophy: runners up 1978/79, 1979/80 (Bradford Northern)
John Player Trophy: winners 1979/80 (Bradford N)
Yorkshire Cup: runners up 1972/73 (Dewsbury), 1981/82, 1982/83 (both Bradford N)
BBC2 Floodlit Trophy: runners up

Andrew Gregory

Born: August 10, 1961, Wigan, Greater Manchester, England.
Height: 5ft 4in.   *Weight:* 10st 8lb.
Position: Scrum half.
Club: Widnes.
Great Britain Honours
Debut (full): December 1981 v France (in Hull)
(under 24): January 1982 v France (in Leeds)
Appearances (full): five
(under 24): one.
Club Honours
Challenge Cup: winners 1980/81, 1983/84; runners up 1981/82

Premiership Trophy: winners 1981/
82, 1982/83
John Player Trophy: runners up
1983/84
Lancashire Cup: runners up 1981/
82, 1983/84.

Andrew suffered an attack of crip-
pling toothache in the early hours of
the morning before the 1981
Challenge Cup final. But with tooth
duly extracted, the 19-year-old
produced a performance that made
him runner up for the Lance Todd
Award.

Andrew, an aggressive, talkative
player, joined Widnes from Wigan
St. Patricks amateur Rugby League
club in 1979 and soon earned himself a regular scrum half position
after the departure of Reg Bowden
to Fulham. He kicked a record nine
goals in the first round of the
Premiership Trophy against Leeds.
The previous record holder, Kevin
Dick, was on the opposing side!
Amazingly Andrew scored only 14
goals in total all season for Widnes.

He has five Great Britain
appearances to his name, but missed
selection for the 1984 Tests with
France after a couple of disputes
with Widnes in the early part of the
season. He was club leading try
scorer with 15 in the 1982/83
season.

A former BARLA Player of the
Year, he was selected for the 1984
tour of Australasia.

Vince Gribbin

Born: July 1965, Whitehaven,
Cumbria, England.
Height: 5ft 10in.   *Weight:* 12st 0lb.
Position: Winger.
Club: Whitehaven.

Club Honours
Leading points scorer: 1982/83,
1983/84.

Vince had a remarkable first season
at Whitehaven as an 18-year-old.
He joined from amateur side Hen-
singham in July 1982 and that first
season immediately became the
club's leading scorer with nine tries
and 49 goals as the Cumbrians won
promotion to Division One.

Whitehaven returned to the
Second Division the next season, but
Vince maintained his form, scoring
tries in five consecutive matches.

Clive Griffiths

Born: April 2, 1954, Loughor, South
Wales.
Height: 5ft 10in.   *Weight:* 13st 1lb.
Position: Full back, centre, wing.
Club: St. Helens.
Welsh Honours
Debut: January 1980 v France (in
Widnes)
Appearances: two as sub.
Club Honours
Top points scorer: 1980/81 season.

When Clive joined St. Helens for
£25,000 in 1979 from Llanelli, he
became the most expensive player to
move from Union to League.

The schoolteacher had played for
the Welsh schools RU side, and the
British Colleges side before joining
Llanelli in 1971. While at Llanelli
he played for Wales once coming on
as a replacement for J. P. R.
Williams – and scoring a try – in
1979.

He took a while to settle into the
pro game, although he was St.
Helens leading points scorer, with
148 points, in the 1980/81 season.

Paul Grimes

Born: September 25, 1960,
Newcastle-upon-Tyne, Tyne and
Wear, England.
Height: 6ft 3in.   *Weight:* 16st 0lb.
Position: Prop forward.
Club: St. Helens.
Club Honours
Division Two: winners 1977/78
(Leigh)
Challenge Cup: winners 1970/71
(Leigh)
Lancashire Cup: winners 1970/71
(Leigh)
BBC Floodlit Trophy: winners 1969/
70, 1972/73 (Leigh); runners up
1976/77 (Leigh).

Paul came down from Newcastle in
1969 for a trial with Leigh following
a newspaper advertisment for new
players. A year later he was winning the first of his four major honours with the club – the Floodlit
Trophy.

The following season was the best
in Paul's 15-year career. After helping Leigh win the Lancashire Cup
he added a Wembley Cup final winners medal against Leeds. Paul
moved to Salford in the 1972/73
season, but could not settle at the
Willows and switched back to Leigh.
Another move came in 1979, when
he went up to Cumbria to join
Whitehaven for £8,000, and in
October 1982 he went to St. Helens
for £12,000. But his future at
'Saints' is not certain, as he was on
the transfer list towards the end of
the 1983/84 season.

Roy Haggerty

Born: March 22, 1960, St. Helens,
Merseyside, England.
Height: 5ft 11in.   *Weight:* 13st 0lb.
Position: Centre.

Club: St. Helens.
Club Honours
Lancashire Cup: runners up 1982/
83.

Roy had his best season for St.
Helens in 1982/83 when he was club
leading try scorer with 18. It earned
him an international call up for the
Test match against France at Carcassonne. He did not play in that
match, but was selected for the 1983
summer squad in readiness for the
1984 Tests.

He is a former groundsman at
St. Helens, the predecessor to Neil
Holding.

Neil Hague

Born: September 7, 1953, Leeds,
West Yorkshire, England.
Height: 5ft 11in.   *Weight:* 13st 4lb.
Position: Utility back.
Club: Leeds.
Club Honours
Challenge Cup: winners 1976/77,
1977/78
Premiership Trophy: winners 1978/
79
John Player Trophy: runners up
1982/83
Yorkshire Cup: winners 1975/76,
1976/77, 1979/80, 1980/81.

When Neil gained representative
colours with Yorkshire in 1977/78 it
was widely predicted international
honours were inevitable. They
never came. But Neil was compensated by the honours won at club
level with Leeds, four Yorkshire
Cups, a Premiership Trophy, and
two winning appearances at Wembley.

Neil played a significant part in
Leeds' success in the 1978
Challenge Cup. First, he scored a

Neil Hague

vital try in the 14-9 semi final victory over Featherstone and second, in the final itself, he laid on the pass for David Smith's 55th minute try which sparked the Leeds revival. A product of the Leeds Supporters club team, Neil fulfilled a lifetime ambition when he signed for the senior team in 1973. At first he had to act as understudy to such great players as Syd Hynes, Les Dyl and John Holmes.

Colin Hall
Born: June 18, 1956, Broughton
　Moor, Maryport, Cumbria,
　England.
Height: 5ft 8in.　*Weight:* 11st 0lb.
Position: Half back.
Club: Whitehaven.

Club Honours
Promotion from Division Two:
　1980/81 and 1982/83.

Colin a signing from Cockermouth Amateur Rugby League team, has spent all his professional career with Whitehaven. He was a former county player as an amateur and is recognised as an accomplished half back, but he has never shone outside his native Cumbria. He established himself as a Whitehaven regular after Arnie Walker retired.

Dave Hall
Born: January 14, 1954, Hull,
　Humberside, England.
Height: 6ft 0in.　*Weight:* 13st 6lb.
Position: Loose forward.

Club: Hull Kingston Rovers.
Great Britain Honours
Debut (full): January 1984 v France
(in Avignon)
(under 24): November 1976 v
France (at Hull KR)
Appearances (full): two
(under 24): one as sub.
Club Honours
Division one: winners 1978/79,
1983/84
Challenge Cup: winners 1979/80;
runners up 1980/81
Premiership Trophy: winners 1980/
81, 1983/84
John Player Trophy: runners up
1981/82
Yorkshire Cup: runners up 1980/81
BBC Floodlit Trophy: winners 1977/
78; runners up 1979/80.

A product of Hull Kingston Rovers'
juniors, Dave has spent all his
professional career with them and
shared the club's great revival of the
late 1970's and early 1980's.

He started his Rovers' career as a
centre before moving to full back,
from where he kicked four goals in
Rovers 26-11 victory over St. Helens
in the 1977/78 Floodlit final. He
later reverted to centre, but now
plays loose forward.

In his first full season he was
selected for the Great Britain under
24 side against France at Craven
Park in 1976 and came on as substitute for the last three minutes.
He was chosen for the full team for
the two Test matches in 1984.

He returned to his centre role for

David Hall

the 1983 Premiership Trophy match against Castleford and scored a Premiership record four tries in Rovers' 35-14 victory. A lover of all sports, Dave has won a Duke of Edinburgh Award.

Lyn Hallett

Born: October 8, 1957, Beddow, Glamorgan, Wales.
Height: 5ft 6in.   *Weight:* 11st 7lb.
Position: Full back.
Club: Cardiff City.
Club Honours
Leading goalscorer: 1983/84 season.

After a slow start to his career, Lyn showed his full potential in 1983/84, becoming the club's top goals and points scorer.

He signed from Steve Fenwick's old club, Bridgend RUFC, in October 1981, and is something of a drop goal expert. He kicked eight in 1982/83, and last season that figure was 29, surpassing Arnie Walker's League record of 22 drop goals in a season.

Steve Hampson

Born: 1963, Newton le Willows, Lancashire, England.
Height: 5ft 9in.   *Weight:* 11st 4lb.
Position: Full back.
Club: Wigan.
Club Honours
Challenge Cup: runners up 1983/84.

After helping Wigan to the 1984 Challenge Cup final at Wembley Steve was robbed of his big chance, when he broke his leg in two places in a league match. What made it even more disappointing for the 20 year old full back thrust into league stardom after being signed from the obscurity of Vulcan Sports Rugby Union club, was that his contribution to the Wigan Wembley effort had been outstanding.

Steve, a Lancashire Colts player, began as a hooker and moved to scrum half before switching to full back. Swinton were the first professional side to notice him and he was offered professional terms after two 'A' team games with them.

Before signing, however, he was given a trial by Wigan and after a brilliant performance, chose to join them instead. Steve signed in November 1983. Two days later he made his first team debut in the John Player Trophy match against York.

Ellery Hanley

Born: March 27, 1961, Leeds, West Yorkshire, England.
Height: 5ft 11in.   *Weight:* 13st 7lb.
Position: Stand off.
Club: Bradford Northern.
Great Britain Honours
Debut (full): January 1984 v France (in Avignon)
(under 24): January 1982 v France (in Leeds)
Appearances (full): one (one as sub)
(under 24): two.
Club Honours
Yorkshire Cup: runners up 1981/82.

Hailing from Leeds, Ellery is one of the young breed of players who had a meteoric rise to fame in the 1980's. He made his Bradford Northern debut in August 1981, scoring one try in the 33-5 Yorkshire Cup victory over Halifax at Thrum Hall. The following January he represented the Great Britain under 24 side against France at Headingly and at the end of that first season he was

Martin Herdman

Northern's leading points scorer with 127 and top try scorer with 15. Towards the end of the 1982/83 season he was in dispute with the club and transfer listed at £75,000. But with the problems resolved, his career took an upward turn in 1984 when he made his full Great Britain debut – coming on as substitute for Joe Lydon in the first test against France at Avignon. He was also selected for the tour of Australasia. He gained a runners up medal in the 1981/82 Yorkshire Cup final when he kicked one goal in the 10-5 defeat by Castleford. An all-round sportsman, Ellery enjoys basketball, volleyball, soccer and table tennis.

Martin Herdman

Born: July 24, 1956, Chertsey, Middlesex, England.
Height: 6ft 2in.   *Weight:* 15st 7lb.
Position: Second row forward.
Club: Fulham.
Wales Honours
Debut: March 1981 v England (Hull KR)
Appearances: two (one as sub).
Club Honours
Division two: winners 1982/83.

Martin was the first Londoner to sign for Fulham, joining from local Amateur Rugby League team, Peckham, on Boxing Day 1980. He also became their first try scorer in the First Division, when he went over in their second match in the top flight against Warrington in September 1981. He spent a period at the end of 1984 on loan at Leigh. Martin, who started in rugby union is also an excellent boxer and a brown belt at karate. He was South West London ABA heavyweight champion in 1978, 1979 and 1980. He also represented England in internationals against Kenya and Hungary. Nowadays Martin enjoys a game of golf, or playing the guitar.

Steve Hesford

Born: May 12, 1954, Luan Sha, Zambia.
Height: 6ft 2in.   *Weight:* 13st 7lb.
Position: Full back/winger.
Club: Warrington.
Club Honours
Premiership Trophy: runners up 1976/77
John Player Trophy: winners 1977/78, 1980/81; runners up 1978/79
Lancashire Cup: winners 1980/81, 1982/83
Man of the Match awards:
    John Player Trophy final
    1977/78 Lancashire Cup 1982/83.

Steve is a member of the unique sports family, Hesford. Father Bob was Huddersfield Town goalkeeper in the 1938 F.A. Cup final – and on the receiving end of the legendary George Mutch's last-minute penalty. Steve's two brothers Iain and Bob are, respectively, a Football League goalkeeper and an England international rugby union forward.

Steve joined Warrington from Fylde Rugby Union club – Bill Beaumont's old team – and made his League debut against Wakefield in November 1975, when he kicked two goals. They were the first of

more than a thousand goals he has kicked for Warrington. And in the Challenge Cup first round tie with Huddersfield, in January 1984, he scored his 2,298th point for the club, beating Brian Bevan's old record.

That record is one of many Steve has set. There was the club record 170 goals in the 1978/79 season and his seven goals and 17 points in the 1980 Lancashire Cup final against Wigan, which created two records for the competition. He was the League's top goal scorer and points scorer in the 1980/81 season and his 130 goals in the First Division in 1978/79 is a record for that Division since the League was reorganised in 1973. Steve has appeared in six senior finals for Warrington (winning four), scoring at least two goals in each of them for a total of 20 goals and two dropped goals.

One of Steve's best performances came in the 1977/78 John Player Trophy final. Underdogs to a strong Widnes side, Warrington won 9-4 with Steve kicking three match-winning goals. One of the most underrated players in the game, Steve kicked 100 goals during 1983/84 for the eighth consecutive season.

David Hobbs

Born: September 13, 1958, Hemsworth, West Yorkshire, England.
Height: 6ft 1in.   *Weight:* 15st.
Position: Second row forward.
Club: Featherstone Rovers.
Great Britain Honours
Debut (full): January 1984 v France (in Avignon)
    (under 24): January 1982 v France (in Leeds)
Appearances (full): two
    (under 24): two.

Club Honours
Second Division Champions: 1979/
80
Challenge Cup: winners 1982/83
Awards: Lance Todd award –
winner 1982/83.

David has had a memorable career
since making his debut for the Great
Britain under 24 team at Leeds in
January 1982 – when he scored two
goals in the 19-16 victory over
France. That season he notched 21
tries in 32 matches for Featherstone
to establish a record for a Featherstone forward.

David is also a proficient goalkicker. He landed seven in his two
under 24 appearances and in his
second appearance for the full Great
Britain side in the second Test
against France at Headingly in
1984, he kicked five in the 10-0
victory.

David started with Featherstone's
Juniors and had his first taste of
representative football when touring Australia and New Zealand
with the British Amateur Rugby
League Association under 18 squad.
In 1984 he was selected for another
tour Down Under. The highlight of
David's career was the 1983
Challenge Cup final at Wembley,
when Featherstone beat the mighty
Hull side. David, a 33-1 outsider
before the match to win the Lance
Todd Man of the Match Award, lifted the trophy with the two tries
that put Featherstone on their way
to a 14-12 victory.

Phil Hogan

Born: October 10, 1954, Barrow in
Furness, Cumbria, England.
Height: 6ft 0in.   *Weight:* 14st 7lb.
Position: Centre.

Club: Hull Kingston Rovers.
Great Britain Honours
Debut (full): June 1977 v France (in
Auckland – World Cup)
(under 24): October 1978 v
Australia (in Hull)
Appearances (full): six (three as sub)
(under 24): two.
Club Honours
Division one: winners 1978/79,
1983/84 (Hull KR)
Divison Two: winners 1975/76
(Barrow)
Challenge Cup: winners 1979/80
(Hull KR); runners up 1980/81
(Hull KR)
Premiership Trophy: winners 1980/
81 (Hull KR)
John Player Trophy: runners up
1981/82 (Hull KR)
Yorkshire Cup: runners up 1980/81
(Hull KR)
BBC Floodlit Trophy: runners up
1979/80 (Hull KR).

When Phil joined Hull Kingston
Rovers in a record £35,000 deal in
December 1978, he hoped it would
bring him the club honours he
had missed at Barrow. He did not
have long to wait in his opening
season. Rovers were First Division
champions for the first time in their
history.

The next season Phil was at Wembley in the Challenge Cup final, and
yet again he struck gold as Rovers
beat Hull in the final. A return visit
in 1981 brought defeat by Widnes,
but Phil was compensated with a
Premiership Trophy winners' medal
– scoring one try in his side's victory
over Hull in front of a near 30,000
crowd at Headingley.

Phil's career began with Barrow
in July 1971, when he was not quite
17. With them he won the Second
Division title in 1975/76. Barrow

came straight back down again, but some of Phil's performances were good enough to earn him selection for the Great Britain World Cup squad in 1977, and on his debut – in the match against France at Auckland – he won the Man of the Match award. His under 24 debut came a year after his senior introduction, when he captained the side against Australia at Craven Park Hull, which, two months later, became his new home.

Keith Holden

Born: 1966, Wigan, Greater
    Manchester, England.
Height: 5ft 7in.   *Weight:* 10st 7lb.
Position: Scrum half.
Club: Wigan.

Only 18, Keith has gained a lot of experience in his short time in the game, but that is not surprising considering his pedigree. Dad, also Keith, is a former Great Britain Test player, who appeared for Warrington, Wigan, St. Helens and Blackpool Borough, in the days of Eric Ashton, Mick Sullivan, Billy Boston and Brian McTigue, Keith senior turned out in two Challenge Cup finals.

Keith junior was a summer signing in 1983 and held down the scrum half position until Gary Stephens was brought back into the side. Great Britain selectors chose him for the two Colts matches with the French 'juniors' in 1983, although he only made the substitutes bench in both matches.

Neil Holding

Born: December 15, 1960, St.
    Helens, Merseyside, England.

Height: 5ft 7in.   *Weight:* 11st 10lb.
Position: Scrum half.
Club: St. Helens.
Great Britain Honours
Debut: (under 24): January 1979 v
    France (in Limoux)
Appearances: (under 24): four.
Club Honours
Lancashire Cup: runners up 1982/
    83.

Scrum half Neil signed for St. Helens on his 17th birthday, having previously been an England schoolboy international.

He has since appeared for the Great Britain under 24 – scoring a try, and kicking a drop goal on his debut in 1979. Neil was selected for the Great Britain 1984 tour of Australasia. Neil spends all his time at Knowsley Road, for when not training or playing, he is the club's groundsman.

Neil is a member of the successful Sunday Mirror Rugby League Roadshow, which tours the country raising money for player's benefits. He is an excellent mimic and, in his younger days, appeared in television's talent show, Junior Showtime.

Les Holliday

Born: August 8, 1962, Whitehaven,
    Cumbria, England.
Height: 6ft 0in.   *Weight:* 13st 12lb.
Position: Loose forward.
Club: Swinton.

Son of former Great Britain player and current Swinton assistant coach, Bill Holliday, Les is showing promise as loose forward.

He joined Swinton from local amateur side Folly Lane in the summer of 1982, and in his first season

Neil Holding

scored four tries in 17 appearances. He highlighted his scoring talent in 1983/84 season with a hat trick in the game with Doncaster at Station Road.

John Holmes

Born: March 21, 1952, Leeds, West Yorkshire, England.
Height: 6ft 0in.   *Weight:* 13st 8lb.
Position: Stand off/full back.
Club: Leeds.
Great Britain Honours
Debut (full): November 1971 v New Zealand (in Leeds)
Appearances (full): 14 (six as sub).
Club Honours
Challenge Cup: winners 1976/77, 1977/78; runners up 1970/71, 1971/72
Premiership Trophy: winners 1974/75
John Player Trophy: winners 1972/73, 1983/84; runners up 1982/83
Yorkshire Cup: winners 1970/71, 1972/73, 1973/74, 1975/76, 1976/77, 1979/80, 1980/81
Championship Play Off: winners 1971/72; runners up 1972/73
BBC Floodlit Trophy: winners 1970/71
Man of the Match Awards: White Rose Trophy – Yorkshire Cup 1972/73 1972/73.

John, a former Captain of Yorkshire schoolboys and the Leeds and District under 17 and under 18 sides, joined Leeds from Kirkstall Boys Club in 1968 – on April Fool's Day. He has since played a record number of games for them – well over 550. In a career with Leeds which has stretched over 15 years, John has won all the major trophies. One of his early successes was helping Leeds win the Floodlit Trophy in

1970/71. Then aged 18, he kicked two goals in the 9-5 victory over St. Helens.

Originally a full back, John made his international debut against New Zealand in front of his home crowd in November 1971 as a 19 year old. He came up against them again twelve months later in the World Cup in Pav, New Zealand and scored 26 points in Britain's 53-19 win. His ten goals made him only the third player – behind Lewis Jones and Bernard Ganley – to kick ten in a match for Great Britain. John went back down under for the 1975 World Cup as a member of the England squad, by which time he had assumed his new role as stand off – a role he played so effectively in Leeds' two Challenge Cup victories in 1977 and 1978.

Even after ten years in the game, John's International career was far from over. He made another Australasian tour in 1977 and in 1979 he came into the Great Britain squad as a late replacement for Warrington's Ken Kelly. In 1982 John's experience was again called upon to help the Great Britain team after their disastrous first Test with Australia. But he could not prevent the Kangaroos from inflicting yet another hefty defeat on the British team, and he made his farewell – and 20th – Great Britain appearance at Wigan in November. At club level he continued to add to his already lengthy total of honours in 1983/84, when Leeds beat Widnes in the John Player Trophy final. That made it 14 senior cup winners medals for John, including seven Yorkshire Cup victories from seven appearances.

Lynn Hopkins

Born: February 13, 1956, Crynant, Glamorgan, South Wales.
Height: 5ft 11in.   *Weight:* 12st 11lb.
Position: Full back.
Club: Workington Town.
Club Honours
Leading goalscorer: 1980/81, 1981/82, 1982/83, 1983/84 (Workington Town).

The 1981/82 season was a record-smashing time for Lynn. His 186 goals for Workington beat the old club record by 48 and his 438 points for the season were a staggering 132 more than the previous club best. He scored in all but one of Workington's games that season, the first against Huyton. His goals and points total including 23 tries put him top of the League lists and he eclipsed Steve Quinn's Second Division points record.

His chance as a goalkicker came with the departure of Iain Mac-Corquodale to Fulham in 1980. He was listed by Workington at £40,000 in the summer of 1983 and snapped up by the ambitious Kent Invicta club. But half way through the season he returned north as the Maidstone based club could not afford the hire purchase repayments of his fee.

Soon after returning to Workington he advised the club he was having three weeks off to go and enjoy the Spanish sunshine! He had acquired a milk business and before starting to develop it wanted to take wife, Diane, on holiday. The club readily agreed, happy that now Lynn has bought the business his roots will be firmly fixed in Cumbria.

Terry Hudson

Born: December 23, 1950, Featherstone, West Yorkshire, England.
Height: 5ft 9in.   *Weight:* 13st 0lb.
Position: Scrum half, loose forward.
Club: Featherstone Rovers.
Club Honours
Division Two: winners 1979/80 (Featherstone Rovers)
Challenge Cup: winners 1982/83 (Featherstone Rovers)
Yorkshire Cup: runners up 1969/70, 1970/71 (Featherstone Rovers).

The great moment in 'Tex' Hudson's lengthy career came at Wembley Stadium on 7th May 1983. Then he held aloft the Rugby League Challenge Cup after Featherstone had brought off a major surprise in beating Hull 14-12. Terry started his career at Featherstone, but moved to Humberside to join Hull KR for £7,000 in 1972.

At Craven Park his game improved and he gained representative honours with Yorkshire. But he eventually lost his place and joined Wakefield. Once again he lost his place – to former England Rugby Union international Mike Lampkowski – and after a brief loan spell at Batley he returned to Featherstone in 1979. He helped them take the Second Division title in 1979/80 – and then came the Wembley success. It was Terry's brilliant performance in the semi-final against Bradford – it won him the Man of the Match award – that took Rovers to that cup final place. Earlier in the season Terry had turned down a £1,000 move to Huddersfield.

Eric Hughes

Born: October 17, 1950, Widnes,
Cheshire, England.
Height: 6ft 0in. *Weight:* 13st 0lb.
Position: Stand off.
Club: Widnes.
Great Britain Honours
Debut (full): October 1978 v
Australia (in Wigan)
Appearances (full): eight.
Club Honours
Division One: winners 1977/78
Challenge Cup: winner 1974/75,
1978/79, 1980/81, 1983/84;
runners up 1975/76, 1976/77,
1981/82
Premiership Trophy: winners 1981/
82, 1982/83; runners up 1977/78
John Player Trophy: winners 1975/
76, 1978/79; runners up 1974/75,
1977/78, 1979/80, 1983/84
Lancashire Cup: winners 1974/75,
1975/76, 1978/79, 1979/80;
runners up 1981/82, 1983/84
BBC Floodlit Trophy: winners 1978/
79; runners up 1973/74.

When Eric stepped out for Widnes in
the 1984 Challenge Cup final
against Wigan, he was appearing in
his 24th major final for the Cheshire
side and a record seventh Wembley
Cup final.

Fast, elusive, and versatile, Eric
is a former P.E. teacher who joined
Widnes in 1969. He had enjoyed
success as a schoolboy Rugby Union
player, representing Lancashire
under 15's and under 19's and also
playing for the England under 15
side. His speed was such that he ran
for Lancashire schoolboys in the 220
yards. After a few mediocre years at
Naughton Park, Eric and Widnes
grew up together and was an inspiration of the side which became
such a power in the mid-seventies.

He has won every honour at club

level: the First Division Championship, four Challenge Cup finals, two
Premiership Trophies, two John
Player Trophies, four Lancashire
Cups, and one Floodlit Cup. Eric's
dynamic play earned him selection
for the England team that took part
in the 1975 World Championships.
He made his Great Britain debut in
1978 and toured Australasia in
1979. His loyalty at Naughton Park
was rewarded with a benefit in
1979. Three years later he scored
the 200th try of his career in the
match with Leeds. A company director, Eric enjoys athletics, swimming
and 'do-it-yourself'.

David Hulme

Born: February 6, 1964, Widnes,
Cheshire, England.
Height: 5ft 7in. *Weight:* 12st 3lb.
Position: Scrum half/stand off
Club: Widnes.
Club Honours
Challenge Cup: 1982/83
Premiership Trophy: winners 1982/
83.

David joined Widnes from Halton
Hornets amateur side in August
1980 and on the departure of Reg
Bowden to Fulham became Andrew
Gregory's understudy. He would be
first choice scrum half or stand off at
most other clubs. He toured Papua
New Guinea and Australia with
Great Britain Colts in 1982. A year
later he was selected as substitute
for the Premiership Trophy final
against Hull in 1983. He came on to
replace Gregory as Widnes went on
to become the first club from outside
the top four to win the Trophy. As
Widnes made their way to yet
another Wembley final in 1984,
David won his first Challenge Cup

winners' medal after coming on as second half subsitute.

Gary Hyde

Born: February 28, 1960,
    Castleford, West Yorkshire,
    England.
Height: 6ft 1in.   *Weight:* 14st 0lb.
Position: Centre.
Club: Castleford.
Great Britain Honours
Debut (under 24): – November 1980
    v New Zealand (in Fulham)
Appearances: (under 24): one (one
    as sub).
Club Honours
Premiership Trophy: runners up
    1983/84
Yorkshire Cup: winners 1981/82;
    runners up 1983/84.

An electrician with the National Coal Board, Gary turned professional with Castleford, his home town club, in 1978, having previously played with their under 17, under 18 and Colts teams.

A free scoring centre, he landed one of the tries in the 1981/82 Yorkshire Cup final which brought Castleford victory over Bradford Northern. He had made two great Britain under 24 appearances and has high hopes of adding to that tally.

In January 1982, he equalled the Division One scoring record with 28 points in a game with Warrington – but saw it broken three months later by John Woods.

Peter Jarvis

Born: December 20, 1945,
    Wetherby, West Yorkshire,
    England.
Height: 5ft 11in.   *Weight:* 15st 7lb.

Position: Coach.
Club: Bramley.
Club Honours
Division Two: runners up 1978/79
    (New Hunslet).

A former prop forward, Peter joined Bramley in 1981 and took over as coach in December 1983, just before a financial crisis had forced the club out of action for a couple of months. Then a new consortium took over and gave Peter the job of coach on a temporary basis. The club was lying fourth from bottom of the Second Division, but by the end of the season they were in a respectable mid-table position.

Highlight of the season was Bramley's performance in the first round of the Challenge Cup, when they held eventual finalists Wigan to a 10-10 draw before going down in the replay at Central Park.

Dick Jasiewicz

Born: April 27, 1958, Batley, West
    Yorkshire, England.
Height: 5ft 10in.   *Weight:* 14st 0lb.
Position: Prop forward.
Club: Bradford Northern.
Great Britain Honours
Debut (full): February 1984 v
    France (in Leeds)
Appearances (full): one.
Club Honours
Yorkshire Cup: runners up 1981/82,
    1982/83.

Great Britain gave a poor display despite beating France in the second Test at Headingley in February 1984. But one bright spot that emerged was the new second row combination of Featherstone's David Hobbs and Bradford's Dick Jasiewicz. Hobbs was playing in his Second test; Jasiewicz was making his debut.

Dick's selection for the Great Britain side in 1984 compensated for his lack of success at club level and the disappointment of losing two Yorkshire Cup finals in successive years, against Castleford and Hull. Jasiewicz signed for Northern from Batley Victoria A.R.L. on October 7, 1980, and played four games that season. The next season he appeared in 15 matches and scored his first try in the opening game of the season, a Yorkshire Cup tie against Halifax. He established himself as a regular in 1982/83 season, missing only three of Bradford's 43 games.

A former bodybuilder he is employed at a health and fitness club.

Barry Johnson

Born: May 31, 1960, Castleford,
   West Yorkshire, England.
Height: 5ft 10in.   *Weight:* 14st 6lb.
Position: Prop forward.
Club: Castleford.
Great Britain Honours
Debut (under 24): January 1982 v
   France (in Leeds)
Appearances (under 24): two.
Club Honours
Yorkshire Cup: winners 1981/82.

Another in the long line of good class youngsters to have been produced by Castleford, Barry played with the Castleford Supporters side between 1975 and 1978 before turning professional.

A former Yorkshire schoolboy player and Great Britain under 18 BARLA player, he was honoured with the captaincy of the Great Britain under 24 side on his debut in

Barry Johnson

1982. Employed as a clerical officer, he lists his hobbies as golf, tennis, and collecting rugby programmes. Castleford captain for the 1983/84 season, he had a bad time with injuries.

He broke his jaw twice during the season, first in the opening match and then on January 1, shortly after making his comeback.

Ken Jones

Born: February 22, 1962, Leigh,
   Greater Manchester, England.
Height: 5ft 9in.   *Weight:* 12st 0lb.
Position: Winger.
Club: Swinton.

Club Honours
Leading goals and points scorer:
1982/83, and 1983/84 seasons.

A capture from Leigh RUFC in November 1981, Ken showed his ability by kicking 20 goals in that first season. The following year saw him end up as the club's leading goalkicker and points scorer with 110 and 253 respectively. He also scored 11 tries – the third highest. His total of 110 goals put him seventh in the League list – the first Swinton player to figure in the top ten since Ken Gowers in 1971/72. Not quite as many goals came in 1983/84 as Swinton pushed for promotion, but Ken still managed to head the club's goals and points list again as well as finishing in the top three try scorers.

John Joyner

Born: March 15, 1955, Leeds, West Yorkshire, England.
Height: 6ft 0in.   *Weight:* 13st 10lb.
Position: Centre.
Club: Castleford.
Great Britain Honours
Debut (full): November 1978 v Australia (in Bradford)
(under 24): December 1976 v France (in Albi)
Appearances (full): fourteen
(under 24): four (one as sub).
Club Honours
Premiership Trophy: runners up 1983/84
John Player Trophy: winners 1976/77
Yorkshire Cup: winners 1977/78, 1981/82; runners up 1983/84
BBC2 Floodlit Trophy: winners 1976/77.

John has worked his way up

John Joyner

through the junior ranks at Castleford to play 14 times for the Great Britain side.

A fast centre, he has scored many vital tries for his club, particularly in the 1976/77 John Player final victory over Blackpool and the 10-5 triumph over Bradford Northern in the 1981/82 Yorkshire cup. When he scored against Bradford Northern in February 1984, he became the tenth player to have scored 100 tries in First Division rugby. He also holds the record for scoring the most tries – five – in one John Player Cup match .... against amateur side Millom in the 1973/74 competition. He was selected for the 1984 Australasia tour.

Vince Karalius

Born: October 15, 1932, Widnes, Cheshire, England.
Height: 6ft 0in.   *Weight:* 14st 8lb.

Position: Manager/coach.
Club: Widnes.
Great Britain Honours
Debut (full): July 1958 v Australia
(in Sydney)
Appearances (full): 12.
Club Honours
Division One: winners 1952/53,
1958/59 (both St. Helens)
Challenge Cup: winners 1955/56,
1960/61 (both St. Helens) 1963/64
(Widnes) 1974/75 (Widnes–
coach) 1983/84 (Widnes–
Manager/coach)
John Player Trophy: runners up
1974/75, 1983/84 (both Widnes–
Manager/coach)
Championship Play-off: winners
1958/59 (St. Helens)
Lancashire Cup: winners 1953/54,
1960/61, 1961/62 (all St. Helens)
1974/75 (Widnes–coach); runners
up: 1956/57, 1958/59, 1959/60 (all
St. Helens) 1977/78 (Wigan–
coach) 1983/84 (Widnes–
Manager).

Nicknamed 'The Wild Bull of the
Pampas' because of his determined
approach to the game, Vince was
born and bred in Widnes. He played
for West Bank juniors before by-pas-
sing the Widnes ground – which was
only ten minutes from his home – to
join St. Helens. Widnes' former
coach Peter Lyons had joined the
Saints a month or so earlier and
recommended Karalius.

Vince made his St. Helens debut
on April 2, 1952 against Warrington
at Knowlsey Road in front of 13,000
fans. Saints won, and the youngster
received rave notices. He rose
through the ranks to captain the
great Saints team of the late fifties
and early sixties and gained two
Challenge Cup winners medals with
them. But he was sacked as skipper

in 1962, replaced by Alex Murphy,
transfer listed at £8,000 and six
weeks later joined his home town
team of Widnes for £4,500. He won a
further Cup winners medal with
them in 1964, when as captain he
gave a brilliant performance in the
13-5 defeat of Hull KR.

Vince, who has established a
scrap business with his brother in
Widnes, hung up his boots to concentrate on the development of the
Company. But he was coaxed back
out of retirement to coach Widnes
for a spell in the mid-seventies and
in 1975 he was back at Wembley for
the fourth time. His opposing coach,
in charge at the Warrington team,
was his old St. Helens team mate,
Alex Murphy. Vince made it four
Challenge Cup wins out of four and
Alex tasted defeat for the first time
in five trips to Wembley. After the
final Vince again announced his retirement to concentrate on business,
but this time Wigan lured him back
in 1977 for a short spell, during
which time he led them to the Lancashire Cup final.

For a third time Vince retired,
and in May 1983, for a third time
came back to take charge at Widnes
as manager, with Harry Dawson as
coach. The pair led the side to the
Lancashire Cup final and John
Player Trophy final – but experienced rare defeats. Harry resigned
in March 1984, but Vince continued
to take the team to Wembley and
another victorious meeting with
Wigan and Alex Murphy.

Now living on the Isle of Man,
Vince published his autobiography
in 1964. It was entitled Lucky 13 –
the number shirt he used to wear
and the address of the house in
which he was brought up – 13, Hood
Lane, Widnes.

Andy Kelly

Born: 1961, Wakefield, West
  Yorkshire, England.
Height: 6ft 2in.   *Weight:* 15st 6lb.
Position: Second row forward.
Club: Hull Kingston Rovers.
Club Honours
Division one: winners 1983/84 (Hull
  KR); runners up 1982/83 (Hull
  KR).

Andy became the most expensive
forward in the game when Hull Kingston Rovers paid Wakefield Trinity
£60,000 for him in 1982. He scored
ten tries in his first season at
Craven Park as Rovers finished runners up in the first division. The try
scoring touch deserted Andy last
season but he still played an important part in Rovers' push for the
first division title.

Ken Kelly

Born: September 7, 1952, St.
  Helens, Merseyside, England.
Height: 5ft 7in.   *Weight:* 10st 10lb.
Position: Stand off/scrum half.
Club: Warrington.
Great Britain Honours
Debut (full): February 1972 v
  France (in Toulouse)
Appearances (full): four.
Club Honours
Division Two: winners 1973/74
  (Bradford Northern)
Challenge Cup: winners 1971/72
  (St. Helens)
Championship Play-off: runners up
  1971/72 (St. Helens)
John Player Trophy: winners 1977/
  78, 1980/81 (Warrington);
  runners up 1978/79 (Warrington)
BBC2 Floodlit Trophy: winners
  1971/72 (St. Helens)
Lancashire Cup: winners 1980/81,
  1982/83 (Warrington)

Awards: Trumanns Man of Steel
  and Trumanns Division One
  Player of the Year – 1981.

This all action half back, one of the
most complete professionals in
modern Rugby League, was almost
lost to the game. He was an accomplished Soccer player at school – one
of his team mates was former Manchester United defender Tommy
O'Neill – and Ken almost made that
sport his living. Instead he joined St.
Helens as a Colt and during 1971/72
season was promoted to the senior
team which won the Challenge Cup
and the Floodlit Trophy.

All that happened before Ken was
20 and in 1973 Bradford Northern
persuaded St. Helens to sell him for
£10,000. But the move was not beneficial and Ken quit the game for a
spell. His exile ended in 1977 when
he was signed by Warrington.
Together they made three John
Player Trophy finals in four years –
twice as winners in 1978 and 1981 –
and two Lancashire Cup final
appearances.

Internationally, Ken has been
a fleeting figure. He has played
four times for Great Britain, the
last against the all-conquering
Australians in 1982. His first Test
jersey came in 1972 and would certainly have had more but for injury.
He was selected for the Great
Britain team to tour Australia and
New Zealand in 1979, but only days
before the team's departure he
broke his jaw in a match against
Bradford Northern.

In 1980/81 he became the first
player to win the Trumanns Man of
Steel award and the First Division
Player of the Year title in the same
year. He relaxes by playing golf and
snooker.

Gary Kemble

Gary Kemble

Born: August 23, 1956,
  Christchurch, New Zealand.
Height: 6ft 2in.   *Weight:* 12st 7lb.
Position: Full back.
Club: Hull.
New Zealand Honours
Debut (full): 1980 v France (in
  Perpignan)
Appearances (full): four.
Club Honours
Division one: winners 1982/83
  (Hull)
Challenge Cup: winners 1981/82
  (Hull); runners up 1982/83 (Hull)
Premiership Trophy: runners up
  1981/82, 1982/83 (both Hull)
Yorkshire Cup: winners 1982/83,
  1983/84 (both Hull).

One of the world's outstanding full
backs, Gary returned to British
shores in 1981 for his second
attempt at English Rugby. He first
came over from New Zealand during
the 1978/79 season to help New
Hunslet win promotion to the First
Division. He went home to play for
Ellerslie, but in 1980 was back as a
member of the touring Kiwis. He
made seven tour appearances, although he was not selected for the
Tests.

After lengthy negotiations in
1981, Hull secured Gary's services.
Since he moved to the Boulevard he
has appeared in two Challenge Cup
finals – scoring one of the tries that
beat Widnes in the 1982 replay –
two Premiership Trophy finals, and
two Yorkshire Cup finals. He also
gained a Championship winners
medal in 1982/83. He has played 20
times for New Zealand including
four Tests and has scored nine tries
and kicked 18 goals.

Shaun Kilner

Born: March 25, 1961, Leeds, West
   Yorkshire, England.
Height: 5ft 8in.   *Weight:* 12st 1lb.
Position: Full back.
Club: Bramley.
Club Honours
Leading scorer: 1982/83, 1983/84.

A first class goal kicker and sound
defender, Shaun has been a life long
supporter of Bramley, at one time he
served them as a ball boy. He has
more than 200 goals to his credit
and was the club's leading kicker
and points scorer in the 1982/83
season, with 104 and 223 respectively. His 104 goals put him in eighth
place in the League list. He was
Bramley's top scorer again in 1983/
84 and his total included a seven
goal haul in the match with Huyton
at McLaren Field.

Bill Kirkbride

Born: February 28, 1946,
   Workington, Cumbria.
Height: 6ft 1in.   *Weight:* 15st 0lb.
Position: Coach.
Club: Rochdale Hornets.
Club Honours
Division one: winners 1973/74,
   1975/76 (Salford) Division two:
   winners 1980/81 (York – coach)
Challenge Cup: winners 1969/70
   (Castleford); runners up 1978/79
   (Wakefield T – coach)
John Player Trophy: runners up
   1972/73 (Salford)
Man of the Match awards: 1970
   Lance Todd Award

Bill took over as coach of struggling
Rochdale Hornets in 1982. Of the
three clubs he has coached so
far, they were the only one with
which he has not enjoyed first

season success. He took charge at
Wakefield in 1979 and within a few
months was leading them out at
Wembley. And his first season at
York saw him win the Second Division title. A second row forward in
his playing days, Bill won the
Challenge Cup with Castleford in
1970 and earned the Lance Todd
Man of the Match award for his
performance. Bill's career started at
Workington Town in 1963. He made
stays at Halifax, Castleford and Salford before joining Wakefield.

Mike Lampkowski

Born: January 4, 1953, Scunthorpe,
   Lincolnshire, England.
Height: 5ft 8in.   *Weight:* 14st 2lb.
Position: Scrum half/loose forward.
Club: Wakefield Trinity.
Club Honours
Challenge Cup: runners up 1978/79.

This former England Rugby Union
international turned professional
with Wakefield Trinity in 1977,
joining them from Headingley
RUFC.
   The nearest Mike has come to
winning an honour in the professional game was in 1979. His fine
performance destroyed St. Helens in
the Challenge Cup semi final and
Wakefield were back at Wembley
for the first time in 12 years. The
wide open space of Wembley seemed
sure to suit his style. Instead, he
was thwarted by the quick thinking
Reg Bowden and Widnes ran out 12-
3 victors. Nicknamed 'Lamb Chop'
Mike was capped at Scrum half for
England four times at Union level.
His League career has been restric-
ted by injuries.

Steve Lane

Born: January 24, 1954, Castleford,
  West Yorkshire, England.
Height: 5ft 6in.   *Weight:* 11st 0lb.
Position: Stand off.
Club: Kent Invicta.
Club Honours
Promotion from Division Two: 1982/
  83 season (Whitehaven)
Hunslet leading try scorer: 1980/81
Whitehaven joint leading try scorer:
  1982/83.

The much travelled Steve has
played his Rugby League all over
the North of England, with Kent
Invicta in the south, and across the
channel with French sides Roanne
and Tonniens.

His career began at Hull, then he
was leading try scorer for Hunslet in
1980/81 with 18, but he played only
a handful of games the following
season and, after loan spells at
Halifax and Bramley, joined Whitehaven in December 1981 for £7,000.
He was Whitehaven's joint top try
scorer with 12 the next year, before
leaving to join the newly formed
Kent Invicta for £8,000.

Kent reorganised themselves
shortly after the start of their first
season and Steve was appointed
player/coach. After a non-too-happy
season at the Maidstone-based club,
Steve resigned as coach in the close
season and was put on the transfer
list.

Barrie Ledger

Born: January 19, 1962, St. Helens,
  Merseyside, England.
Height: 5ft 11in.   *Weight:* 11st 8lb.
Position: Winger.
Club: St. Helens.
Great Britain Honours
Debut (under 24): November 1983 v

France (in Villeneuve)
Appearances (under 24): two.
Club Honours
Lancashire Cup: runners up 1982/
  83.

Like his father before him, Barrie is
a winger with his home town club of
St. Helens. He signed in February
1981, having made his way through
the Colts team. In the 1982/83
season he scored 14 tries and earned
selection for the Great Britain
under 24 side. St. Helens are going
through a transitional period with
the emphasis on youth and Barrie is
an important part of that rebuilding.

Martin Lee

Born: March 2, 1961, Leigh, Greater
  Manchester, England.
Height: 5ft 7in.   *Weight:* 10st 6lb.
Position: Scrum half.
Club: Swinton.
Club Honours
Leading try scorer: 1982/83 season.

Martin, Swinton's leading try scorer
in his first full season of 1982/83
with 16, joined them from Leigh
East Amateur Rugby League club in
February 1982.

His try scoring last season was a
significant factor in Swinton's
challenge for a First Division place.
He scored a hat trick against Dewsbury in January and four against
Keighley in April.

James Leulai

Born: 1957, Auckland, New
  Zealand.
Height: 6ft 0in.   *Weight:* 13st 4lb.
Position: Winger.
Club: Hull.
New Zealand Honours

Debut (full): 1979 v Great Britain
Appearances (full): 15.
Club Honours
Division One: winners 1982/83
Challenge Cup: winners 1981/82;
  runners up 1982/83
Premiership Trophy: runners up
  1981/82, 1982/83
John Player Trophy: winners 1981/
  82
Yorkshire Cup: winners 1982/83,
  1983/84
Awards: New Zealand Player of the
  Year – 1983.

An explosive runner with the ball,
James returned to his try scoring
ways with Hull during the 1982/83
season, after suffering injury during
the match with the 1982 touring
Australians. The New Zealander
will be remembered for his memorable try in the Challenge Cup semi-
final against Castleford. It was a
brilliant solo effort in which he sped
past two Castleford defenders,
swerved round a third, and then
double sidestepped the full back
before sprinting to the line. Leulai
toured with the Kiwis in 1980, and
12 months later was back to join
Hull. He has been a prominent
member of the highly successful
Hull side since then and has won all
the major domestic honours – with
the exception of the Premiership
Trophy.

Wally Lewis

Born: December 1, 1959, Brisbane,
  Australia.
Height: 5ft 11in.   *Weight:* 14st 7lb.
Position: Stand off.
Club: Wakefield Trinity.
Australian Honours
Debut (full): 1981 v France
Appearances (full): nine.

Australian Wally, reputed to be the
world's best stand off, joined Wakefield Trinity for part of the 1983/84
season at a fee of £1,000 per match.
But he had to leave in February
1984, with them heading for relegation from the First Division to
return to Brisbane ready for the new
season there with Wynnum-Manly.
Vice captain on the Kangaroos
1982/83 tour of Britain, Wally is a
delicatessen owner, who enjoys
scuba diving, sky diving and skiing.

Graham Liptrot

Born: July 8, 1955, St. Helens,
  Merseyside, England.
Height: 5ft 10in.   *Weight:* 12st 12lb.
Position: Hooker.
Club: St. Helens.
Great Britain Honours
Debut (under 24): November 1977 v
  France (in Hull)
Appearances (under 24): four.
Club Honours
Division one: winners 1974/75
Challenge Cup: runners up 1977/78
Premiership Trophy: winners 1976/
  77
Lancashire Cup: runners up 1982/83
BBC2 Floodlit Trophy: runners up
  1977/78, 1978/79.

Graham has played more than 300
games for St. Helens since joining
them from Colts rugby in 1973. He
had won representative honours for
Lancashire Schoolboys at under 15,
under 17 and under 19 level, as well
as playing for Great Britain at
under 19.
Originally understudy to Tony
Karalius at Knowsley Road, he
claimed the hooker's spot before the
end of 1973 and was in the team
that finished runners up in the First
Division. Graham toured Australia

Graham Liptrot

and France with his club in 1976 and the following year made the first of his four Great Britain under 24 appearances. He was selected by England for his matches with France and Wales in 1979 and these sound performances put him in the Great Britain squad for their summer tour. But he did not play in any of the internationals and senior selection is not likely to come his way again.

Nicknamed 'Lippy', he is married to the daughter of former Great Britain centre Eric Ashton.

Sammy Lloyd

Born: September 11, 1951, Allerton Bywater, Near Castleford, West Yorkshire, England.
Height: 5ft 11in. *Weight:* 14st 4lb.
Position: Second row.
Club: Hull.

Club Honours
Division one: winners 1982/83 (Hull) Division two: winners 1978/79 (Hull)
Challenge Cup: winners 1981/82 (Hull); runners up 1979/80 (Hull)
Premiership Trophy: runners up 1981/82 (Hull)
John Player Trophy: winners 1976/77 (Castleford)
Yorkshire Cup: winners 1977/78 (Castleford)
BBC2 Floodlit Trophy: winners 1976/77 (Castleford).

A fast second row forward, Geoff Lloyd – known as 'Sammy' – is also a deadly goal kicker. He holds the club record at both Castleford and Hull for most goals and most points in a season. Also, for most goals in one match – 17 for Castleford against Millom in 1973 and 14 for Hull against Oldham in 1978. In that game against Millom he scored 43 points in the match – another club record and the third highest individual score in one match in Rugby League history. He also kicked a record five goals in the 1977/78 Yorkshire Cup final against Featherstone and was the first player to land 500 Division One goals since the re-introduction of the two Division system.

A product of Fryston juniors, Sammy joined Castleford on 25th November 1968. He has never represented his country, however, apart from being travelling substitute with the England squad and a non playing member of the 1977 Great Britain World Cup squad. His defensive play does not match up to his goal kicking skills. He moved to Hull for £12,000 in August 1978 and won Second and First Division titles with them. He also played in the

Sammy Lloyd

1982 Wembley Challenge Cup final against Widnes but missed the replay at Elland Road. He has been transfer listed by Hull and could retire soon. He enjoys swimming and golf.

Brian Lockwood

Born: October 8, 1946, Castleford, West Yorkshire, England.
Height: 5ft 11in.　*Weight:* 15st 7lb.
Position: Coach.
Club: Huddersfield.
Great Britain Honours
Debut (full): October 1972 v Australia (in Perpignan – World Cup)
Appearances (full): eight (one as sub).
Club Honours
Division One: winners 1978/79 (Hull KR)
Challenge Cup: winners 1968/69, 1969/70 (both Castleford), 1979/80 (Hull KR), 1980/81 (Widnes)
Premiership Trophy: winners 1981/82 (Widnes)
Lancashire Cup: runners up 1981/82 (Widnes)
Yorkshire Cup: runners up 1968/69, 1971/72 (both Castleford)
Championship Play-off: runners up 1968/69 (Castleford)
BBC Floodlit Trophy: runners up 1979/80 (Hull KR)
Man of the Match Awards: Lance Todd award – Challenge Cup final 1979/80.

Along with Alex Murphy, Brian holds the distinction of having gained Challenge Cup winners' medals at Wembley with three different clubs. He won with his home town club Castleford in 1969 and 1970, and ten years later he was back for a third with Hull KR. He added the fourth with Widnes in 1981 at the age of 34.

A product of the Castleford junior side, Brian signed for them in 1963 and stayed for 14 years. Apart from those two Cup winners medals he appeared in three other finals with them – a Championship Play-off defeat by Leeds in 1969 and Yorkshire Cup final defeats in 1968 and 1971 by Leeds and Hull KR.

Brian made his Great Britain debut in the 1972 World Cup in France against Australia, Great Britain went on to win the Cup. A spell playing in Australia improved his game.

He moved to Wakefield Trinity in 1977, taking over as coach for a while, before moving to Hull Kingston Rovers in 1978. The transfer rejuvenated his career. He was soon back in a Great Britain jersey, after an absence of four years and in the second Test against Australia at

Odsal on 5th November 1978 he won the Man of the Match award in the 18-14 victory. At the end of his first season with Rovers they were First Division champions. The following year they were runners up in the Floodlit final and back at Wembley. Brian's third Challenge Cup appearance brought a third winners' medal and the Lance Todd Man of the Match award. He made it four out of four with Widnes in 1981. Brian took charge of the once great Huddersfield side as coach in 1983, and at the same time he runs the Sun Inn in Loftus, near Wakefield.

Phil Lowe

Born: January 19, 1950, Hull, Humberside, England.
Height: 6ft 2in.   *Weight:* 16st 4lb.
Position: Coach.
Club: York.
Great Britain Honours
Debut (full): July 1970 v New Zealand (in Auckland)
Appearances (full): 12.
Club Honours
Division One: winners 1978/79 (Hull KR)
Challenge Cup: winners 1979/80 (Hull KR); runners up 1980/81 (Hull KR)
Premiership Trophy: winners 1980/81 (Hull KR)
John Player Trophy: runners up 1981/82 (Hull KR)
Yorkshire Cup: winners 1967/68 (Hull KR); runners up 1980/81 (Hull KR)
Championship Play-off: runners up 1967/68 (Hull KR)
BBC Floodlit Trophy: winners 1977/78 (Hull KR); runners up 1979/80 (Hull KR).

A former basketball, discus and hur-
dles champion at school, Phil also captained the Hull and Yorkshire schoolboys rugby teams before joining Hull Kingston Rovers in 1967. The following year, when only 18, he was in their Championship Play-off team beaten by Wakefield Trinity in the final. That season did not go totally without reward, for Lowe was in the side which beat Hull in the Yorkshire Cup final. It was ten years before Phil won further honours at club level, although he did have a three year spell with Manly in Sydney, Australia, returning in September 1976.

Phil made his international debut on the 1970 tour of Australasia, scoring two tries on his debut against New Zealand. After his return from Sydney, Phil regained his international place and was selected for the 1979 tour, but declined for personal reasons. The late seventies and early eighties produced his most successful spell in the game. He appeared in seven major finals for Rovers – including two Challenge Cups at Wembley – as well as being in the side which won the First Division title in 1978/79. He almost produced a spectacular finale to his first season as York coach in 1983/84. The Second Division club climaxed a remarkable run by losing to Wigan in the Challenge Cup semi final. A publican, Phil is also a crack shot.

Joe Lydon

Born: November 26, 1963, Wigan, Greater Manchester, England.
Height: 6ft 1in.   *Weight:* 12st 6lb.
Position: Winger/centre.
Club: Widnes.
Great Britain Honours
Debut (full): February 1983 v

France (in Carcassonne)
(under 24): January 1983 v
France (in Carpentras)
Appearances (full): three
(under 24): three.
Club Honours
Challenge Cup: winners 1983/84
Premiership Trophy: winners 1982/83
John Player Special Trophy:
runners-up 1983/84
Lancashire Cup: runners up 1983/84
Man of the Match Awards: Lance
Todd award – Challenge Cup,
1984
Awards: Greenalls Man of Steel,
1983/84 Greenalls Division One
Player of the Year 1983/84
Greenalls Young Player of the
Year 1983/84.

Joe had a fairy tale first season at
Widnes in 1982/83. Not only was he
the club's second highest try scorer
with 14, but he also won a Premiership winners' medal thanks to a 22-
10 victory over arch rivals Hull. Joe
kicked five goals in that game. He
gained Great Britain under 24 honours against France, but was given
little opportunity to show his talent
and must have thought his international career would be halted.

Instead, a month later he was
selected for the senior team for the
match against France and
celebrated in fine style. He took over
from club mate Mick Burke as goal
kicker and landed three goals.
There was also a spectacular try
when he latched on to a loose ball
and twice kicked ahead before
touching down.

Joe had originally wanted a
career in Rugby Union after touring
Zimbabwe with England Schoolboys
in 1981. But the powers of per-
suasion from Doug Laughton, the
Widnes coach, convinced him to

Joe Lydon

turn pro in August 1982.

His successful 1983/84 season
came to an end with him not only
collecting his first Challenge Cup
winners' medal, but also the Lance
Todd award. His performance in the
final against Wigan was highlighted by his two tries. The first saw
him run 70 yards before touching
down, and the second 85 yards. Four
days after his Wembley appearance,
Joe swept the board at the Greenalls
Man of Steel presentation, becoming
the first player to win three awards
at one presentation.

A graphic design student at Pres-
ton Polytechnic he is on a special
diet to increase his weight. He
demonstrated his blinding speed
with two of Widnes' match-winning
tries at Wembley in 1984 and was a
success on Great Britain's summer
tour of Australia.

Colin Maskill

Born: March 15, 1964, Wakefield,
   West Yorkshire, England.
Height: 5ft 10in.   *Weight:* 12st 7lb.
Position: Hooker.
Club: Wakefield Trinity.
Great Britain Honours
Debut (under 24): November 1983 v
   France (in Villeneuve)
Appearances (under 24): one.
Club Honours
Division two: runners up 1982/83
   Leading goal scorer: 1982/83,
   1983/84.

At 17, Colin won the Man of the
Match award on his senior debut for
Wakefield against Hull during the
1981/82 season to serve notice on
the Belle Vue fans that he was going
to be an important part of their
future. That first season saw him
make only five senior appearances,
but the following season he was a
regular member of the Trinity side
that won promotion and he ended as
the club's top goal and points scorer,
with 77 and 181 respectively. A
product of the Colts team, he signed
professional two days after his 17th
birthday in 1981.
   In an effort to improve his game
he went to Australia in April 1984,
with team mates Nigel Bell and
Paul Geary. A miner, he relaxes by
fishing.

Roy Mathias

Born: September 2, 1949, Llanelli,
   South Wales.
Height: 6ft 1in.   *Weight:* 14st 7lb.
Position: Winger, second row
   forward.
Club: St. Helens.
Great Britain Honours
Debut (full): June 1979 v Australia
   (in Brisbane)

Appearances (full): one.
Club Honours
Division One: winners 1974/75
Challenge Cup: winners 1975/76;
   runners up 1977/78
Premiership Trophy: winners 1975/
   76, 1976/77; runners up 1974/75
Lancashire Cup: runners up 1982/83
BBC2 Floodlit Trophy: winners
   1975/76; runners up 1978/79.

Roy gained Welsh international
Rugby Union caps at schoolboy,
under 25 and senior level before St.
Helens tempted him away from
Llanelli RUFC in 1972. It did not
take him long to be selected for the
Welsh team, gaining the first of 20
caps in 1975 against France. Later
that year he represented Wales in
the World Championship.
   Roy's best seasons at club level
came in 1975/76 and 1976/77, when
he won the Challenge Cup, the
Premiership Trophy twice, and the
BBC Floodlit Trophy – scoring twice
in the final with Dewsbury. Originally omitted from the 1979 Great
Britain tour squad, he was selected
as replacement for John Bevan and
played his one and only Test in the
first game with Australia at Brisbane, a 35-0 hammering. Away from
Rugby, Roy breed dogs and enjoys
fishing.

Hussein M'Barki

Born: May 29, 1956, Khemisset,
   Morocco.
Height: 5ft 9in.   *Weight:* 12st 4lb.
Position: Winger.
Club: Fulham.
Club Honours
Division Two: winners 1982/83.

Hussein M'Barki – alias Des Smith
– joined Fulham from French side

Cahors in November 1981 in a £25,000 deal. His move to England made him the first Moroccan to play in the Rugby League. A try scorer winger, he notched eight in his first season, and 23 in his first full season – just four behind club record scorer John Crossley.

Mal Meninga

Born: July 8, 1960, Bundaberg, Queensland, Australia.
Height: 6ft 1in.   *Weight:* 15st 10lb.
Position: Centre.
Club: St. Helens.
Australian Honours
Debut: 1982 v New Zealand (in Sydney)
Appearances: nine.
Club Honours
Brisbane Premier Grade: winners 1981; runners up 1982 (Brisbane Souths).

Australian Test centre Mal, one of the finest attacking players in the world, joined St. Helens for the start of the 1984/85 season. His £40,000 contract – with lucrative inventive bonuses - made him the highest paid player in the Rugby League.

Mal, who joins Brisbane Souths team mate Phil Vievers at St. Helens, was recorded top scorer for the Kangeroos in their 1982 tour of Great Britain with 118 points. The Queensland policeman has taken a leave of absence to play in England.

Roger Millward

Born: September 16, 1947, Castleford, West Yorkshire, England.
Height: 5ft 4in.   *Weight:* 11st 0lb.
Position: Coach.
Club: Hull Kingston Rovers.

Great Britain Honours
Appearances (full): 28 (one as sub)
Debut (full): March 1966 v France (in Wigan).
Club Honours
Division one: winners 1978/79 (Hull KR – player-coach) 1983/84 (Hull KR – coach)
Challenge Cup: winners 1979/80 (Hull KR – player-coach); runners up 1980/81 (Hull KR – coach)
Premiership Trophy: winners 1980/81, 1983/84 (Hull KR – coach)
John Player Trophy: runners up 1981/82 (Hull KR – coach)
Yorkshire Cup: winners 1966/67, 1967/68, 1971/72, 1974/75 (all Hull KR); runners up 1975/76 (Hull KR) 1980/81 (Hull KR – coach)
Championship Play-off: runners up 1967/68 (Hull KR)
BBC Floodlit Trophy: winners 1965/66 (Castleford) 1977/78 (Hull KR); runners up 1979/80 (Hull KR – coach).

Roger was a highly respected stand off, known as 'Roger the Dodger' after television commentator Eddie Waring coined the nickname for his darting. He turned pro with his home town team Castleford in 1964 and made his international debut in the Test with France at Wigan in March 1966 when only 18, one of the youngest ever to play for Great Britain.

Shortly afterwards he joined Hull Kingston Rovers for £6,000 and between then and 1980 when he retired, he scored a club record 207 tries. His international career continued to flourish at Craven Park and he made 47 appearances, including 29 Tests for Great Britain. He toured with Great Britain five times, and once with England, and captained both sides in World Cup competitions.

In 1977 he was appointed player-coach at Hull KR in succession to Harry Poole and steered them to Wembley in 1980. He broke his jaw in the match but still managed a smile when he took the trophy from Her Majesty the Queen Mother. Roger broke his jaw again in an A team match with Batley the following October and decided to hang up his boots to concentrate on coaching. He took Hull KR to the First Division/Premiership double in 1983/84 – the first time that double had been achieved.

The former National Coal Board electrician was an excellent long jumper in his younger days, reaching Northern Counties standard. He was made M.B.E. in the 1983 New Years honours list.

Bob Mordell

Born: July 2, 1953, London, England.
Height: 6ft 2in.   *Weight:* 15st 0lb.
Position: Manager.
Club: Kent Invicta.
Club Honours
Division Two: winners 1981/82 (Oldham).

The former Rugby Union international succeeded Bill Goodwin as coach of League newcomers Kent Invicta, after the reorganisation of the club mid way through their first season. Bob had played for Rosslyn Park and gained his one England cap against Wales in 1978. He turned professional in October 1979 with Oldham.

During his first season at the Watersheddings, the club won promotion. Kent signed him before

the start of their first League campaign, paying a club record £13,500.

Mick Morgan

Born: September 30, 1948, Featherstone, West Yorkshire, England.
Height: 5ft 9in.   *Weight:* 13st 0lb.
Position: Prop forward.
Club: Oldham.
England Honours
Debut (full): January 1975 v France (in Perpignan)
Appearances (full): three (three as sub).
Club Honours
Division Two: winners 1979/80 (Featherstone Rovers)
John Player Trophy: runners up 1971/72 (Wakefield Trinity)
Yorkshire Cup: runners up 1973/74, 1974/75 (Wakefield Trinity)
Awards: Trumanns Man of Steel Second Division Player of the Year – 1982.

A student of the game in more ways than one, Mick often takes part in sports quizzes in the North West. Mick's sporting talents go beyond rugby. He was West Riding Schools Discus Champion in 1959 and is a fine swimmer.

Mick started his League career with Featherstone under 17 team in 1964, but it was nearby Wakefield Trinity who signed him as a 17-year-old. At Wakefield he appeared in a John Player Trophy final and two Yorkshire Cup finals – ending up on the losing side each time. But he did captain the side to the 1973/74 Yorkshire Cup final triumph against Leeds.

He made his debut for England in the 1975 European Championship match with France in Perpignan –

coming on as substitute for Hull KR's, John Millington, in the 76th minute. Five more England appearances followed, four in the World Championships. Mick moved from Wakefield to York, and then to his home town club Featherstone Rovers, whom he helped win the Second Division title in 1979/80. Mick seemed set to spend the rest of his days at Post Office Road, but when Allan Agar took over as coach of newly formed Carlisle, Mick was one of the first players he recruited as assistant coach. He relished the new challenge. In the first season he not only helped Carlisle to promotion, but scored 25 tries, a League record for a prop forward. Mick succeeded Agar as Carlisle coach in July 1982, but after a disastrous first season in the top division, moved on to Oldham.

He is a regular auctioneer with the Sunday Mirror Rugby League Roadshow.

Terry Morgan

Born: October 9, 1956, Pontefract, West Yorkshire, England.
Height: 6ft 1in.   *Weight:* 12st 4lb.
Position: Winger.
Club: York.
Club Honours
Division Two: winners 1980/81 (York)
Yorkshire Cup: runners up 1978/79 (York).

A speedy winger with goalkicking skills, Terry made an £8,000 move from Keighley to York in 1978. Critics of the outlay were soon silenced as Terry quickly gained selection for the Yorkshire county side. Terry's father Dennis played for Bramley, Bradford and Feather-

stone. And Oldham prop Mick Morgan is Terry's uncle. Terry had a brief spell away from Wigginton Road at the beginning of 1982 when he joined Carlisle, on loan. Terry entered York's record books in October 1983. His nine goals and one try against Cardiff gave him 22 points, equalling the club record held jointly by Vic Yorke, Steve Quinn and current colleague, Chris Gibson.

Keith Mumby

Born: February 21, 1957, Spennymoor, County Durham, England.
Height: 5ft 8in.   *Weight:* 12st 7lb.
Position: Full back.
Club: Bradford Northern.
Great Britain Honours
Debut (full): November 1982 v Australia (in Wigan) (under 24): November 1976 v France (in Hull)
Appearances (full): four (under 24): six.
Club Honours
Division One: winners 1979/80, 1980/81
Division Two: winners 1973/74
Premiership Trophy: winners 1977/78; runners up 1978/79, 1979/80
John Player Trophy: winners 1979/80
Yorkshire Cup: winners 1978/79; runners up 1981/82, 1982/83
Man of the Match: Yorkshire Cup Final 1982/83
Awards: Trumanns Man of Steel First Division Player of the Year – 1982/83.

Keith, a former member of the Police Boys' Club team, joined Bradford Northern as a 16-year-old in 1973. He was the last junior Rugby League player to be signed before

Keith Mumby

the age limit was raised to 17. He made a sensational start, scoring a try and kicking 12 goals on his debut. Those goal kicking skills were to earn him the Bradford Northern Player of the Year Award three times before his 21st birthday.

He earned international recognition in 1976 with the Great Britain under 24 side. Three years later, after dazzling displays for England against Wales and France, he was selected for the full Great Britain side to tour Australia. He was kept in reserve that time, however, and it in 1982 that he made his Great Britain debut, against Australia at Wigan when he kicked three goals. For Northern, Keith kicked two goals in their Premiership Trophy win over Widnes in 1978 before nearly 17,000 spectators at Station Road, Swinton.

But the highlight of his career came in January 1984 when he captained Great Britain in the first Test against France at Avignon, in succession to Northern team mate Brian Noble, who was ruled out by suspension. He was further honoured with selection for the 1984 Great Britain touring team, for his second tour.

Keith, record points and goal scorer for Bradford, was voted Trumanns Man of Steel First Division Player of the Year for the 1982/83 season, and will be enjoying his benefit year from November 1984.

Alex Murphy

Born: April 22, 1939, St. Helens, Merseyside, England.
Height: 5ft 9in.   *Weight:* 11st 7lb.
Position: Coach.
Club: Wigan.
Great Britain Honours

Alex Murphy

Debut (full): June 1958 v Australia (in Sydney)
Appearances (full): 27.
Club Honours
Division One: winners 1958/59, 1959/60, 1964/65, 1965/66, (all St. Helens) 1972/73 (Warrington – player-coach) 1981/82 (Leigh – coach)
Challenge Cup: winners 1960/61, 1965/66 (both St. Helens) 1970/71 (Leigh – player-coach) 1973/74 (Warrington – player-coach); runners up 1974/75 (Warrington – coach), 1983/84 (Wigan – coach)
Premiership Trophy: runners up 1976/77 (Warrington – coach)
John Player Trophy: winners 1973/74, 1977/78 (Warrington – coach) 1982/83 (Wigan – coach)
Lancashire Cup: winners 1961/62, 1963/64, 1964/65 (all St. Helens)

1970/71 (Leigh – player-coach)
1981/82 (Leigh- coach); runners
up 1969/70 (Leigh – player-coach)
Championship Play-off: winners
1958/59, 1965/66 (both St.
Helens); runners up 1964/65 (St.
Helens)
BBC Floodlit Trophy: winners 1969/
70 (Leigh – player-coach); runners
up 1965/66 (St. Helens) 1967/68
(Leigh – player-coach) 1974/75
(Warrington – coach)
Man of the Match Awards: Lance
Todd Award – 1970/71 Challenge
Cup final.

One of the game's greatest charac-
ters, Alex won everything there was
to win in a playing career which
spanned nearly 20 years and 575
matches. Then he set about becoming the country's best coach. Alex
signed for his home town club, St.
Helens, on his 16th birthday. At 18
he was rated the best scrum half in
the world and a year later became
the youngest ever Great Britain
tourist. He made his Test debut during the 1958 tour of Australia and
the following March scored a record
four tries in the first Test with
France at Leeds.

After two successful Wembley
appearances and a Championship
Play-off triumph with St. Helens,
Alex moved on in 1967 following a
disagreement. He crossed the East
Lancashire Road to join Leigh as
player-coach and helped them win
the Floodlit Trophy, the Lancashire
Cup final and in 1971, the
Challenge Cup. Alex collected the
Lance Todd Man of the Match
Award.

Controversial as always, he left
the club immediately after the Cup
final to revive struggling Warrington. Yet again, the Murphy magic

had worked. At the end of his second
season, Warrington were League
champions for the first time since
1956. He was back at Wembley in
1974, leading his new club to victory
to become the first man to captain
three different winning sides at
Wembley. A broken jaw ended his
playing career soon afterwards.

He was appointed England coach
in the 1975 World Championships
and just failed to land another title
when England were beaten by Australia in the final reckoning. He
moved to Salford in 1978, endured
two strangely barren years, and returned to Leigh in November, 1980
and straight away took them to the
League Championship.

A month after winning the Championship he was on the move again -
to his present club Wigan, leaving
Leigh with 18 months of a contract
still to run. The controversial
Murphy masterminded a surprise
defeat of Leeds to lift the John
Player Trophy for the first time in
Wigan's history. Last season he
blended a fine mixture of youth and
experience at Central Park to earn
another trip to Wembley against
Widnes. It proved to be his second
defeat at Wembley, and his opposing
coach on both occasions was Vince
Karalius.

Frank Myler

Born: December 4, 1938, Widnes,
Cheshire, England.
Height: 5ft 11in.   *Weight:* 12st 8lb.
Position: Coach.
Club: Great Britain.
Great Britain Honours
Debut (full): September 1960 v New
Zealand (in Bradford – World
Cup)
Appearances (full): 23 (one as sub).

Club Honours
Division One: winners 1977/78
(Widnes – coach)
Division Two: winners 1981/82
(Oldham – coach)
Challenge Cup: winners 1963/64
(Widnes); runners up 1975/76,
1976/77 (Widnes – coach)
Premiership Trophy: runners up
1977/78 (Widnes – coach)
John Player Trophy: runners up
1973/74 (Rochdale H – coach)
1977/78 (Widnes – coach)
Lancashire Cup: winners 1968/69
(St. Helens) 1976/77 (Widnes –
coach); runners up 1970/71 (St.
Helens)
Championship Play-off: winners
1969/70 (St. Helens)
BBC Floodlit Trophy: runners up
1968/69 (St. Helens) 1971/72
(Rochdale H – player-coach)
Awards: Trumanns Man of Steel
Coach of the Year – 1978
Man of the Match Awards: Harry
Sunderland Trophy – 1970
Championship Play-off.

Frank started his career with his
home town side of Widnes as a teen-
ager and soon established himself as
a try scorer. In 1958/59 he scored 34,
which still stands as a club record
for a season.

Frank made his Great Britain
debut in the 1960 World Cup and
ten years later he was playing in the
competition again. He toured with
Great Britain twice and was captain
in all six Tests in 1970 – the last
Ashes victory. He moved from Widnes to nearby St. Helens in 1967 for
four years, before taking up his first
coaching job, as player-coach to
Rochdale Hornets in 1971 Frank led
them to the John Player final in
1974, where they were beaten by
Warrington, and to the 1971/72

Floodlit final, where they went
down 8-2 to St. Helens. In 1976 he
landed the plum position as coach of
his first club, Widnes. He guided
them to four finals but they won
only one – the 1976 Lancashire Cup.
They did however, take the First
Division title in 1977/78, a performance which won Frank the
Trumanns Coach of the Year
Award.

Frank retired to concentrate on
his business, but was tempted back
by Swinton. He moved to Oldham in
May 1981, and the following season
led them to the Second Division
title. He quit Oldham in April 1983
to take the Great Britain job and the
1984 tour of Australia.

John Myler

Born: March 7, 1958, Widnes,
Cheshire, England.
Height: 5ft 10in.   *Weight:* 13st 3lb.
Position: Utility player.
Club: Widnes.
Great Britain Honours
Debut (under 24): January 1982 v
France (in Leeds)
Appearances (under 24): one (one as
sub).
Club Honours
Challenge Cup: winners 1980/81.

Brother of fellow Widnes player
Tony Myler, John is also the nephew
of current Great Britain coach
Frank Myler. He has played in
every back position for Widnes, as
well as turning out at loose forward,
and although unable to command a
regular place during the past couple
of seasons, is a valued squad
member.

He has appeared in only one
major final, but it was one to re-
member. He came on as substitute

John Myler

Club Honours
Challenge Cup: runners up 1981/82
Premiership Trophy: winners 1981/
82, 1982/83
Lancashire Cup: runners up 1983/84
Man of the Match Awards: Harry
Sunderland Trophy – 1983
Premiership Trophy.

The world of Tony Myler was temporarily shattered after ten minutes of the Challenge Cup semi-final with Leeds at Swinton in March, 1984. As Widnes powered their way to another Wembley appearance, Tony limped off with a torn knee cartilage. The injury, at first sight, ruled him out of the Cup final and the Great Britain summer tour. He underwent surgery immediately and astounded the medics by gaining selection for the Great Britain tour led by his uncle, Frank.

Tony joined Widnes from Widnes RUFC in 1978. He made his under 24 Great Britain debut in 1982 and, 12 months later, was a key figure in the two senior Tests with France. Tony's finest game in a Widnes shirt was the 1983 Premiership Trophy final against Hull. He dominated the game winning a unanimous vote for the Harry Sunderland Man of the Match Trophy.

Tony's brother John is a team mate at Naughton Park.

in the 1981 Challenge Cup final to replace Eddie Cunningham and then climbed the steps to the Royal Box to collect his winners medal following the 18-9 defeat of Hull KR. The following January he made the first of his two Great Britain under 24 appearances, again as substitute. He came on to replace his Widnes team mate, full back Mick Burke and impressed so much he was retained for the return match against France.

Tony Myler
Born: September 26, 1960, Widnes,
Cheshire, England.
Height: 6ft 0in.   *Weight:* 11st.
Position: Stand off
Club: Widnes.
Great Britain Honours
Debut (full): February 1983 v
France (in Carcassonne)
(under 24): February 1982 v
France (in Tonneins)
Appearances (full): two
(under 24): three.

Steve Nash
Born: April 7, 1949, Featherstone,
West Yorkshire, England.
Height: 5ft 5in.   *Weight:* 11st 2lb.
Position: Scrum half.
Club: Salford.
Great Britain Honours
Debut (full): March 1971 v France
(in St. Helens)
Appearances (full): 24.

Club Honours
Division One: winners 1975/76
(Salford)
Challenge Cup: winners 1972/73
(Featherstone Rovers); runners
up 1973/74 (Featherstone Rovers)
Premiership Trophy: runners up
1975/76 (Salford)
Lancashire Cup: runners up 1975/76
(Salford)
Yorkshire Cup: runners up 1969/70
(Featherstone Rovers)
Man of the Match Awards: Lance
Todd Award – 1972/73 Challenge
Cup Final
Awards: Trumanns Man of Steel
Second Division Player of the
Year – 1983.

Steve was born in Post Office Road –
home of Featherstone Rovers and
signed for them in February 1967,
after appearing in their under 17
and under 19 teams. His enthusiasm was the backbone of the
great Featherstone revival, which
saw them make successive trips to
Wembley in 1973 and 1974. The
first was the more memorable for
Steve – not only did he come away
with a winners' medal, but also the
Lance Todd Award for his outstanding performance, capped by a
cheeky 71st minute dropped goal.
Steve made his international bow at
St. Helens in 1971 and in 1974 made
the first of four tours to Australia.
He has gone on to win 24 Great
Britain caps and was sent off during
the 1978 Test with Australia.

He moved to Salford in 1975 for a
record £15,000 and immediately
helped them to the First Division
title. He was given a benefit by
Salford in 1984, after more than 300
games for them. Away from the
game, Steve enjoys photography,
shooting, pop music, and sports cars.

Brian Noble

Born: February 14, 1961, Bradford,
West Yorkshire, England.
Height: 5ft 8in.   *Weight:* 13st 0lb.
Position: Hooker.
Club: Bradford Northern.
Great Britain Honours
Debut (full): November 1982 v
Australia (in Leeds)
(under 24): January 1982 v
France (in Leeds)
Appearances (full): four
(under 24): four.
Club Honours
Division one: winners 1980/81
Yorkshire Cup: runners up 1981/82
Awards: Trumanns Man of Steel
Young Player of the Year – 1982/
83.

Since turning professional on his
17th birthday, Brian has made a
dramatic rise and captained Great
Britain in the Second Test against
France at Headingley in February,
1984.

In fact he had been nominated as
captain for the first Test three
weeks earlier, but he was banned by
a disciplinary hearing held three
days before the game. Brian had
shown his leadership by steering the
under 24 side to a 48-1 win over
France the previous December. He
proved himself again in that second
Test with a 10-0 victory. Brian was
vice captain on the 1984 Great
Britain tour of Australia and New
Zealand, replacing Trevor Skerrett
who withdrew from the party.

Noble began with the Bradford
Schools XIII. He joined West York-
shire Police Force and played with
their Colts team as well as Bradford
Northern Colts and Great Britain
Colts.

David Noble

Born: April 29, 1957, Wakefield,
West Yorkshire, England.
Height: 5ft 10in.   *Weight:* 13st 0lb.
Position: Utility back.
Club: Doncaster.
Club Honours
Leading points scorer in career
(Doncaster) Most goals in career
(Doncaster) Most points in a
season: 1982/83 (Doncaster).

David broke the three club records
for Doncaster in 1982/83. First he
passed David Towies' record of 240
goals in a career when he kicked his
241st in the home game with Batley
on September 15. Then on October
24 his try against Huyton was
his 505th point for the club, again
beating Towies' record. Finally,
with the last kick of the season he
notched his 188th point, taking him
one point beyond Tyssul Griffiths'
21 year old mark.

David started his career at Doncaster and made moves to Wakefield
Trinity and Hull, before returning
to Tatters Field in August 1980. He
is a former Great Britain Colts international.

Steve Norton

Born: December 22, 1951,
Castleford, West Yorkshire,
England.
Height: 5ft 11in.   *Weight:* 14st 1lb.
Position: Loose forward.
Club: Hull.
Great Britain Honours
Debut (full): July 1974 v Australia
(in Sydney)
Appearances (full): 11 (one as sub).
Club Honours
Division One: winners 1982/83
(Hull)
Division Two: winners 1978/79

(Hull)
Challenge Cup: winners 1981/82
(Hull); runners up 1979/80, 1982/
83 (both Hull)
Premiership Trophy: runners up
1980/81, 1981/82, 1982/83 (all
Hull)
John Player Trophy: winners 1976/
77 (Castleford) 1981/82 (Hull)
Yorkshire Cup: runners up 1971/72
(Castleford) 1979/80 (Hull)
BBC Floodlit Trophy: winners 1976/
77 (Castleford), 1979/80 (Hull)
Awards: Trumanns Man of Steel
Second Division Player of the
Year – 1979, and First Division
Player of the Year – 1982.

Frustrated by injuries, Steve
announced his retirement in
November 1983. But he was back in
the Hull team before the end of the
season helping them in their
challenge for a second successive
First Division title.

Steve, once regarded as the
world's best loose forward, joined
Castleford from local junior side
Fryston in October 1968. His rise in
senior football was meteoric. After
only two first team games he was
pitched into the 1970 Challenge Cup
semi-final between Castleford and
St. Helens. Steve signed for Hull on
January 25, 1978 for £25,000 and
his first game attracted their
highest gate of the season. Hull
were relegated, but after one season
in the Second Division bounced back
as champions with a 100% record.
The revival had begun and since
then Steve has won most of the
games honours at club level. He was
also voted the Trumanns Man of
Steel as Player of the Season in both
the First and Second Divisions – the
only player to have won both
honours.

Dane O'Hara

Dane O'Hara

Born: 1956, Auckland, New
  Zealand.
Height: 5ft 11in.   *Weight:* 12st 11lb.
Position: Winger.
Club: Hull.
New Zealand Honours
Debut (full): 1977 v France.
Appearances (full): 20.
Club Honours
 Division one: winners 1982/83
Challenge Cup: winners 1981/82;
  runners up 1982/83
Premiership Trophy: runners up
  1981/82, 1982/83
John Player Trophy: winners 1981/
  82
Yorkshire Cup: winners 1983/84.

Dane was a star of the 1980 New
Zealand tour of Britain. The leading
try scorer with six, his style of play
attracted enquiries from Feather-

stone and Hull KR. But it was KR's
neighbours Hull who tempted him
over from Glenora in June 1981. In
his first game Dane punctured a
lung and was out for a month. He
returned to help Hull beat Hull KR
12-4 in the John Player Trophy and
then play a crucial role in the
Challenge Cup final. Dane scored
Hull's try nine minutes from the
end, which levelled the scores at 14-
14 and forced the replay which Hull
won.

Dane, the most capped of current
New Zealand internationals with 20
Test appearances since 1977,
became Kiwi captain in succession
to Mark Graham.

Kevin O'Loughlin

Born: February 25, 1947, Wigan,
  Greater Manchester, England.
Height: 5ft 11in.   Weight: 13st 0lb.
Position: Utility.
Club: Unattached.
Club Honours
League Championship: winners
  1970/71 (Wigan)
Challenge Cup: runners up 1969/70
  (Wigan)
Championship Play-off: runners up
  1970/71 (Wigan)
BBC2 Floodlit Final: winners 1968/
  69 (Wigan); runners up 1969/70
  (Wigan)
Lancashire Cup: winners 1971/72,
  1973/74 (both Wigan).

Although a product of Warrington
Colts Kevin turned professional
with nearby Wigan in 1963. He
spent 17 years there, playing alongside some of the great post war stars
like Ray Ashby, Billy Boston, Eric
Ashton and Brian McTigue.

Wigan were League Champions
in 1971 and a Lancashire Cup

winners medal came Kevin's way the following season when Wigan beat Widnes. Two years later he played one of the most memorable matches, scoring two tries in the County final. Kevin, brother of Widnes winger Kieron O'Loughlin, moved to Swinton in 1980, and was released at the end of the 1984 season.

Kieron O'Loughlin

Born: March 13, 1953, Wigan, Greater Manchester, England.
Height: 5ft 11in.   *Weight:* 12st 8lb.
Position: Winger.
Club: Widnes.
Club Honours
Challenge Cup: winners 1983/84 (Widnes); runners up 1981/82 (Widnes)
Premiership Trophy: winners 1981/82 (Widnes)   ial
John Player Special Trophy: runners up 1983/84 (Widnes)
Lancashire Cup: winners 1973/74 (Wigan); runners up 1983/84 (Widnes).

Now a veteran, Kieron was making headlines a decade ago when, a 21-year-old, he scored two tries in Wigan's 19-9 defeat of Salford in the Lancashire Cup final. From Wigan he moved to Workington and then in November 1981 to Widnes for £30,000. Kieron earned them a Wembley appearance in his first season with a sensational last-minute try in the Challenge Cup semi-final win over Leeds at Swinton. He followed up a Mick Adams' up and under and touched down after the ball had bounced off the cross bar. Widnes lost the cup to Hull after a draw at Wembley. But revenge followed the week after as Widnes beat Hull in the Premiership Trophy final.

Now in his thirties, Keiron is still a key member of Widnes first team squad, his opening try in the 1984 Challenge Cup final paving the way to yet another Widnes Wembley triumph. His brother Kevin, who was with Kieron at Wigan, played for Swinton during 1983/84.

Mike O'Neill

Born: November 29, 1960, Widnes, Cheshire, England.
Height: 6ft 1in.   *Weight:* 14st 0lb.
Position: Prop forward.
Club: Widnes.
Great Britain Honours
Debut (full): November 1982 v Australia (in Leeds)
(under 24): November 1980 v New Zealand (in Fulham)
Appearances (full): three
(under 24): three (two as sub).
Club Honours
Challenge Cup: winners 1978/79, 1980/81, 1983/84; runners up 1981/82
Premiership Trophy: winners 1979/80, 1981/82, 1982/83
Lancashire Cup: runners up 1981/82.

Mike joined Widnes from local amateur side Widnes Tigers in 1977. The former Great Britain Colts international sprang to prominence during the 1978/79 season and in May 1979 was selected as substitute for the Challenge Cup final against Wakefield Trinity. Still only 18, he replaced Alan Dearden and collected a winners' medal following the 'Chemics' 12-13 success.

Mike has gone on to play for Great Britain at under 24 and senior level.

Mike O'Neill

He made his Test debut against the Australians in the third Test at Leeds in 1982.

A former athletics champion at school, he gained Lancashire and Merseyside under 16 honours at Rugby Union. Brother Steve is a team mate at Widnes.

Steve O'Neill

Born: February 1, 1958, Widnes, Cheshire, England.
Height: 5ft 10in.   *Weight:* 14st 8lb.
Position: Front row/second row.
Club: Widnes.
Great Britain Honours
Debut (under 24): January 1979 v France (in Limoux)
Appearances (under 24): two.
Club Honours
Challenge Cup: runners up 1981/82 (Widnes)

Premiership Trophy: winners 1982/ 83 (Widnes) John Player Special Trophy: runners up 1983/84 (Widnes)
Lancashire Cup: runners up 1980/81 (Wigan) 1983/84 (Widnes).

A strong forward, Steve started his career at Wigan, despite being born in Widnes. He became a first team regular in 1978 and, shortly after, was in the Great Britain under 24 team.

He moved to Widnes for £26,000 in October 1981 and at the end of his first season was on his way to Wembley.

Widnes lost to Hull in a replay at Elland Road after a draw at Wembley and that losers' medal was one of three he picked up with Widnes before striking gold in 1984.

Mick Parrish

Born: April 19, 1958, Bradford,
  West Yorkshire, England.
Height: 6ft 4in.   *Weight:* 15st 12lb.
Position: Winger.
Club: Oldham.
Club Honours
Division two: winners 1981/82
  (Oldham).

Oldham doubled their transfer
record in September 1980, by paying
Hunslet £20,000 for ace goal kicker
Mick Parrish. And the following
season he repaid them with 164
goals and 379 points.

He scored in every game, a feat he
had performed with Hunslet in
1979/80. He was the first player to
achieve such a record with two clubs
and only one man – the great David
Watkins – had performed the feat
with the same club.

Oldham won promotion as Second
Division champions and Mick has
gone on to become the club's leading
scorer each season since.

Bill Pattinson

Born: July 8, 1954, Cockermouth,
  Cumbria, England.
Height: 6ft 2in.   *Weight:* 13st 7lb.
Position: Second row forward/loose
  forward.
Club: Workington Town.
England Honours
Debut: February 1981 v France (in
  Leeds)
Appearances: one (one as sub).
Club Honours
Lancashire Cup: winners 1977/78;
  runners up 1976/77, 1978/79,
  1979/80.

A speedy forward, Bill has attracted
the interest of big clubs like Wigan
and Hull KR in recent years. He

Mick Parrish

played for the amateur team in Cockermouth where he was born and bred before joining Workington Town in the mid Seventies. He appeared in four consecutive Lancashire Cup finals although only one of them yielded a winners' medal – the 1977 competition in which they beat Wigan 16-13. Bill has represented England twice. He came on as substitute in the European Championship match with France at Leeds in February 1981 and played against Wales at Craven Park, Hull a few weeks later.

Geoff Peggs

Born: August 14, 1941, Keighley,
   West Yorkshire, England.
Height: 5ft 11in.   *Weight:* 13st 7lb.
Position: Coach.
Club: Keighley.

Geoff followed Lee Greenwood as Keighley coach in 1983 and struggled to keep them away from the bottom four in the Second Division. A former player with Bramley and Rochdale Hornets, Geoff coached the British Universities side before taking his first pro job with Keighley.

Clive Pickerill

Born: March 19, 1956, Wakefield,
   West Yorkshire, England.
Height: 5ft 6in.   *Weight:* 11st 1lb.
Position: Scrum half.
Club: Wakefield Trinity.
Club Honours
Challenge Cup: runners up 1979/80
   (Hull)
Yorkshire Cup: winners 1977/78
   (Castleford).

Castleford had two outstanding scrum halves on their books in the

mid-seventies – Gary Stephens and Clive Pickerill. One of them had to lose out and it was Clive.

He decided to move on in 1979 after six years and although he was essentially a reserve, Hull stepped in with a record £20,000. At the Boulevard, he gained a runners' up medal in the Challenge Cup before joining Wakefield Trinity in October 1981.

Harry Pinner

Born: September 26, 1956, St.
   Helens, Merseyside, England.
Height: 5ft 10in.   *Weight:* 13st 1lb.
Position: Loose forward.
Club: St. Helens.
Great Britain Honours
Debut (full): October 1980 v New
   Zealand (Wigan)
   (under 24): November 1976 v
   France (Hull)
Appearances (full): one (one as sub)
   (under 24): four (four as sub).
Club Honours
Challenge Cup: runners up 1977/78
Premiership Trophy: winners 1976/
   77
Lancashire Cup: runners up 1982/83
BBC2 Floodlit Trophy: runners up
   1977/78, 1978/79

The 'king of the drop kick', Harry Pinner has more than 70 to his name since scoring his first against Wakefield Trinity on April 11, 1976. Since then, Harry's one point kicks have won many a match, and none more so than the Challenge Cup second round tie with Hull in 1984 when he dropped four.

Harry joined St. Helens as an amateur international and in his first full season, 1976/77 helped them to the Premiership Trophy. Harry was sent off in the final for

Harry Pinner

Great Britain Honours
Debut (full): June 1977 v France (in
   Auckland)
Appearances (full): four.
Club Honours
Challenge Cup: winners 1976/77,
   1977/78
Premiership Trophy: winners 1974/
   75, 1978/79
Yorkshire Cup: winners 1975/76,
   1976/77, 1979/80, 1980/81
Man of the Match Awards: Lance
   Todd award – 1976/77.

Nicknamed the 'Bionic Barrel'
Steve will never be forgotten for his
Lance Todd winning performance in
the 1977 Challenge Cup final at
Wembley. That nickname, given to
him by the Australians, sums up his
astonishing physique, which wore
down the Widnes defence in that
Cup final and enabled Leeds to win
by 16 points to seven.

Steve joined Leeds from their
Juniors in 1969, but did not make
the breakthrough into first team
football until 1974. But that first
full season saw him produce the
exciting brand of football for which
he has since been known and it was
justice that he ended the year with a
winners medal in the Premiership
Trophy final when Leeds beat St
Helens. Two years – and two Yorkshire Cup winners medals later –
Steve made the first of his two successful Wembley Cup final appearances. The first, not only won him
the Lance Todd award, but also
gained him selection for Great
Britain's World Cup squad. He
played in all four of Britain's
matches in the 1977 World Cup,
including the final in which he
scored one try as Australia took the
trophy by a single point. In all Steve
has won eight major cup winners

fighting with Warrington's Alan
Gwilliam. Harry made his first
appearance in a Wembley Cup final
the following year and despite his
hefty up and under, which led to St.
Helens' first minute try, had to be
content with a runners' up medal.

He was selected for England in
1980 and later that year made his
Great Britain debut, coming on as
substitute for Trevor Skerrett in the
first Test with New Zealand at
Wigan. He was selected for his first
Great Britain tour in 1983/84. A
publican in Newton le Willows,
Harry breeds bulldogs.

Steve Pitchford

Born: February 6, 1952, Hunslet,
   West Yorkshire, England.
Height: 5ft 9in.   *Weight:* 15st 13lb.
Position: Prop forward.
Club: Leeds.

medals, notching up at least one every season from 1974/75 to1980/81. He has never appeared on the losing side in a major club final. He failed to gain a regular place in the Leeds side for a couple of seasons and moved to Wakefield on loan in January 1984.

Although Steve hung up his boots during the 1983/84 season to run a Wakefield pub, friends predict he will soon be back in action.

Andy Platt

Born: October 9, 1963, Billinge, Merseyside, England.
Height: 5ft 11in.   *Weight:* 14st 0lb.
Position: Utility player.
Club: St. Helens.

Andy joined St. Helens from amateurs Wigan St. Patricks in June 1982, after playing for Great Britain under 19 and captaining the BARLA side. He had an impressive first season slotting in as a centre, loose forward or second row. Andy's brother Duncan recently joined Wigan from St. Helens rugby union side, West Park.

Ian Potter

Born: August 6, 1958, St. Helens, Merseyside, England.
Height: 6ft 1in.   *Weight:* 14st 7lb.
Position: Second row/loose forward.
Club: Wigan.
Great Britain Honours
Debut (under 24): January 1979 v France (in Limoux)
Appearance (under 24): four.
Club Honours
Division One: winners 1981/82 (Leigh)
John Player Trophy: winners 1977/78. 1980/81 (both Warrington)

Lancashire Cup: winners 1980/81 (Warrington).

Alex Murphy, one of the shrewdest coaches in the game, has signed Ian Potter three times. Murphy took the former amateur star to Warrington and, following two successes in the John Player Trophy, signed Potter for his new club, Leigh, in September 1981 for £50,000 – a record sum for a forward.

Murphy moved on to Wigan and in February 1984 was back calling for Potter with a £20,000 cheque. Ian, a former soccer trialist with Blackburn Rovers and Liverpool, has been dogged by a series of knee injuries.

Eric Prescott

Born: June 21, 1948, Widnes, cheshire, England.
Height: 6ft 0in.   *Weight:* 14st 3lb.

Eric Prescott

Position: Second row forward.
Club: Salford.
Club Honours
Division one: winners 1973/74,
1975/76 (both Salford)
Challenge Cup: winners 1980/81
(Widnes); runners up 1981/82
(Widnes)
Premiership Trophy: winners 1981/
82, 1982/83 (Widnes); runners up
1975/76 (Salford)
Lancashire Cup: winners 1972/73
(Salford); runners up 1970/71 (St.
Helens), 1973/74, 1974/75, 1975/
76 (all Salford) 1981/82, 1983/84
(both Widnes)
Championship Play-off: winners
1969/70 (St. Helens)
BBC Floodlit Trophy: winners 1971/
72, (St. Helens) 1974/75 (Salford)
runners up 1970/71 (St. Helens).

Eric, one of the best uncapped
players during the seventies, has
been a great ambassador for the
game. He has all round skills and
can play either in the back row or
second row, and is a useful goal
kicker.

He started his career at St. Helens
in 1968 joining them from Widnes
works team I.C.I. and appeared in
four major finals with the Saints. He
gained winners' medals in the Lancashire Cup, Championship Play-off
final and BBC Floodlit Final. But he
was left out of the St. Helens Cup
final team in 1972 and the Championship final team the following
week. Upset, he went to Salford for a
then record £13,500 fee.

During Eric's nine years there, he
won two First Division titles, a Lancashire Cup, and a Floodlit Trophy
in one of the club's most successful
post war eras. Eric joined Widnes for
£20,000 in 1981 and immediately
made the Wembley appearance that

had eluded him at St. Helens.

The blond haired Eric is now back
at Salford after a deal which took
John Wood to Widnes in 1983.

Wayne Proctor
Born: November 20, 1963, Hull,
Humberside, England.
Height: 6ft 1in.   *Weight:* 14st 0lb.
Position: Second row.
Club: Hull.
Great Britain Honours
Debut (under 24): November 1983 v
France (in Villeneuve)
Appearances (under 24): one.
Club Honours
First Division: winners 1982/83
Yorkshire Cup: winners 1983/84.

Wayne, a product of the highly successful Hull colts, made his senior
debut during the 1981/82 season.
The following season he played in
half the club's fixtures, winning a
championship medal. He made his
Great Britain Colts debut in the 10-
8 defeat by France in 1981 and
graduated to the under 24's two
years later.

He was selected for the 1984
Great Britain tour as a replacement.

Gary Prohm
Born: October 1, 1958, Auckland,
New Zealand
Height: 6ft 0in.   *Weight:* 13st 0lb.
Position: Utility player.
Club: Hull Kingston Rovers.
New Zealand Honours
Debut (full): 1978 v Australia
Appearances (full): 15.
Club Honours
Division one: winners 1983/84;
runners up 1982/83
Premiership Trophy: winners 1983/
84.

Gary joined the Kiwi invasion in 1982 when he moved to Hull Kingston Rovers from New Zealand side Mount Albert. At the end of that first season he was joint leading try scorer for Rovers with 17 – the same as Garry Clark. Rovers finished runners up in the First Division and Gary continued to score useful tries in his second season as Rovers went one better and won the title.

He has worn the New Zealand jersey 45 times, 15 in Test matches. In those 45 matches he has scored 20 tries.

Steve Quinn

Born: June 12, 1952, York, North Yorkshire, England.
Height: 5ft 11in.   *Weight:* 13st 7lb.
Position: Centre.
Club: Featherstone Rovers.
Club Honours
Division One: winners 1976/77 (Featherstone Rovers)
Division Two: winners 1979/80 (Featherstone Rovers)
Challenge Cup: winners 1982/83 (Featherstone Rovers)
Yorkshire Cup: runners up 1976/77, 1977/78 (both Featherstone Rovers)
Awards: Trumanns Man of Steel Second Division Player of the Year – 1980.

As York made the drop from the First Division at the end of 1975, the one bright spot was the goalkicking of Steve Quinn. He had landed 112 goals and Featherstone swooped to sign him the following January in an exchange deal for Barry Hollis. Steve made an immediate impact at Rovers, scoring four goals on his debut in the Cup tie with Wakefield

Trinity. He went on to kick a club record 152 goals in his first full season.

Steve has continued to break both club and League records. He was leading First Division goalscorer in 1977 and 1982 (shared with John Woods). He also topped the League's goals and points charts in 1979/80, with 163 and 375 respectively – both club records. His 500 goals and 1,700 points are a Featherstone career best and in one game against Doncaster in the 1979/80 season he scored 29 points – another club record.

Further barriers fell in 1979/80 as he helped Featherstone to the Second Division title. His 332 points were a Second Division record, he kicked 100 goals in the first 18 matches (equalling the feat of Bernard Ganley and David Watkins) and won the Trumanns Man of Steel Second Division Player of the Year award.

Despite it all, Steve must have thought cup honours were going to elude him until 1983 when he kicked four goals as Rovers beat Hull at Wembley.

Dennis Ramsdale

Born: December 23, 1956, Wigan, Greater Manchester, England.
Height: 6ft 1in.   *Weight:* 13st 0lb.
Position: Centre/winger.
Club: Wigan.
Club Honours
Challenge Cup: runners up 1983/84
John Player Trophy: winners 1982/83
Lancashire Cup: runners up 1980/81.

Desperately unlucky with injuries,

Dennis is a skilful winger and one of the best defensive players in the game.

A former Wigan colt, he progressed through the junior ranks to enjoy one of his best seasons in 1980/81. He scored a try in Wigan's Lancashire Cup final defeat by Warrington and went on to become the club's top try scorer for the season with 19.

Alan Rathbone

Born: October 20, 1958,
   Warrington, Cheshire, England.
Height: 6ft 0in.   *Weight:* 13st 9lb.
Position: Loose forward.
Club: Bradford Northern.
Great Britain Honours
Debut (full): November 1982 v
   Australia (in Wigan)
   (under 24): November 1979 v
   France (in Leigh)
Appearance (full): two (one as sub)
   (under 24): one as sub.
Club Honours
Division one: winners 1980/81
   (Bradford Northern)
Division two: winners 1977/78
   (Leigh)
Yorkshire Cup: runners up 1981/82
   (Bradford Northern)

A former loose forward with Leigh and Rochdale Hornets, Alan moved to Bradford Northern in June 1981 and scored a try in his first match, the Yorkshire Cup tie with Halifax two months later. He represented Lancashire and Great Britain at schoolboy and Colts level and was a member of the BARLA under 19 squad.

His under 24 debut came against France in 1979 and his first full cap followed three years later against Australia at Wigan. He has not been as successful at club level. A former amateur boxer, he won 19 of his bouts.

Keith Rayne

Born: May 23, 1956, Wakefield,
   West Yorkshire, England.
Height: 6ft 0in.   *Weight:* 14st 8lb.
Position: Prop forward.
Club: Leeds.
Great Britain Honours
Debut (full): January 1984 v France
   (in Avignon)
   (under 24): November 1979 v
   France (in Leigh)
Appearances (full): two
   (under 24): two.
Club Honours
Challenge Cup: runners up 1978/79
   (Wakefield Trinity) John Player
   Special Trophy: winners 1983/84
   (Leeds).

Keith played with his brother Kevin in the same school team and that association has continued throughout his career. They both joined their home town team of Wakefield Trinity, then moved to Leeds – Keith in September 1980 for £35,000 and Kevin 15 months later. Keith surpassed Kevin in 1979 when he was selected for the Great Britain under 24 side and in 1984 he was a member of the senior team in the first Test against France at Avignon, and also went on to the 1984 tour of Australasia.

Club honours have been scarce for this all round sports enthusiast: only a John Player Special Trophy winners' medal from the 1984 victory over Widnes and a runners' up medal from his Wembley appearance with Wakefield in 1979.

Kevin Rayne

Kevin Rayne

Born: May 23, 1956, Wakefield,
West Yorkshire, England.
Height: 6ft 0in.   *Weight:* 14st 8lb.
Position: Prop forward.
Club: Leeds.
Club Honours
John Player Special Trophy:
winners 1983/84 (Leeds).

Kevin, the twin brother of Great
Britain international Keith, started
his career at Wakefield Trinity in
1974 and was substitute for them in
the 1979 Challenge Cup final defeat
by Widnes.
  A quick thinking prop, he followed his brother to Leeds in December 1981 for a fee of £41,500.

Alan Redfearn

Born: August 31, 1952, Batley, West
Yorkshire, England.
Height: 5ft 7in.   *Weight:* 12st 0lb.
Position: Scrum half.
Club: Bradford Northern.
Great Britain Honours
Debut (full): July, 1979 v Australia
(in Sydney)
Appearances (full): one.
Club Honours
Division one: winners 1979/80,
1980/81
John Player Cup: winners 1979/80
Premiership Trophy: winners 1977/
78; runners up 1978/79, 1979/80
Yorkshire Cup: winners 1978/79;
runners up 1981/82.

This younger brother of former
Bradford Northern and Great
Britain international David Red-
fearn joined Bradford Northern
from local side Shaw Cross in 1971.
He spent several years as under-

study to Barry Seabourne before breaking into the first team.

His most successful period was in the late seventies and early eighties when he gained two First Division championship titles, a John Player Trophy winners' medal and a Yorkshire Cup winners' medal. Those performances earned him selection for the 1979 Australasia tour and he appeared in the third Test at Sydney. He has represented England twice.

A painter and decorator, he is a member of the select band who have scored 100 tries in the First Division.

Mal Reilly

Born: January 19, 1948, Allerton
 Bywater, West Yorkshire,
 England.
Height: 6ft 0in.   *Weight:* 15st 0lb.
Position: Coach.
Club: Castleford.
Great Britain Honours

Mal Reilly

Debut (full): June 1970 v Australia
 (in Brisbane)
Appearances (full): nine.
Club Honours
Challenge Cup: winners 1968/69,
 1969/70
Premiership Trophy: runners up
 1983/84 (coach)
John Player Trophy: winners 1976/
 77 (Player/coach)
Championship Play-off: runners up
 1968/69
Yorkshire Cup: winners 1977/78
 (player/coach) 1981/82 (coach)
 runners up 1968/69, 1983/84
 (coach)
BBC Floodlit Trophy: winners 1967/
 68, 1976/77 (player/coach)
Man of the Match Awards: Lance
 Todd award – 1969 Challenge Cup
 Final
Awards: Trumanns Man of Steel
 Division One Player of the Year –
 1977.

Born in Allerton Bywater near Garforth, Mal joined Castleford from local side Kippax in 1965, and they have been his only club in Britain. He won two successive Challenge Cup winners' medals with them and the Lance Todd award – before emigrating in 1971 to join Sydney team Manly Warringah – for a then world record £15,000 fee. He returned in 1974, guested for Castleford several times and was then offered the player/coach job in December that year.

He is now the longest serving coach in the League. In 1977 he was the first recipient of the Trumanns Man of Steel First Division Player of the Year. But a long-standing knee injury has now almost certainly ended his on-field career.

His hobbies are swimming, fishing, shooting and chess.

Alan Rhodes

Born: July 31, 1948, Castleford,
  West Yorkshire, England.
Height: 6ft 1in.   *Weight:* 13st 4lb.
Position: Coach.
Club: Sheffield.
Club Honours
Challenge Cup: winners 1972/73
  (Featherstone Rovers); runners
  up 1973/74 (Featherstone Rovers)
Yorkshire Cup: runners up 1970/71
  (Featherstone Rovers) 1978/79
  (York)
Captain Morgan Trophy: runners up
  1973/74 (Featherstone Rovers).

A former second row forward with
Featherstone Rovers and York,
Alan was appointed first coach to
the newly elected Sheffield team in
1984. He joined Featherstone in
1968 and appeared in the Challenge
Cup finals of 1973 and 1974. He
moved to York in the mid-seventies
before becoming coach at Doncaster.

Maurice Richards

Born: February 2, 1945, Ystrad,
  Rhondda, South Wales.
Height: 5ft 11in.   *Weight:* 13st 2lb.
Position: Winger.
Club: Salford.
Great Britain Honours
Debut (full): July 1974 v Australia
  (in Sydney)
Appearances (full): two.
Club Honours
Division one: winners 1973/74,
  1975/76
Premiership Trophy: runners up
  1975/76
John Player Trophy: runners up
  1972/73
Lancashire Cup: winners 1972/73;
  runners up 1974/75, 1975/76
BBC2 Floodlit Trophy: winners
  1974/75.

For nearly ten years, Salford fans
were treated to devastating play by
two of the best wingers in the game,
Keith   Fielding   and   Maurice
Richards. Richards, a British Lion,
won nine Welsh caps during his six
years with Cardiff RUFC and
played himself into Welsh folklore
in 1969, when he scored four tries
against England.

He signed for Salford on October
15, 1969 and made his debut for
them the same day at home to
Leigh. The first of his tries came in a
Floodlit   Trophy   match   against
Castleford   and   on   September   5,

Paul Ringer

1982 he scored his 293rd to create a club record. He has also made most appearances for the club, playing his 500th game during the 1983/84 season. During his 15 years at the Willows, Salford have won only two major cup competitions, the Lancashire Cup in 1972/73 and the Floodlit Trophy two seasons later. Maurice scored a try in each final.

Surprisingly, Maurice won his only Great Britain caps on the 1974 tour of Australasia and he has made only two appearances for Wales in the 1975 and 1977 World Championship. Maurice, Welsh junior long jump champion in 1963, is employed as a computer systems analyst.

Paul Ringer

Born: January 28, 1951, Cardigan, Wales.
Height: 6ft 1in.   *Weight:* 14st 7lb.
Position: Second row forward.
Club: Cardiff City.
Welsh Honours
Debut: November 1981 v England (in Cardiff)
Appearances: two.

Welshman Paul, sent off in the Rugby Union international against England at Twickenham in 1980, carried his hard man image over to the professional game and can now claim the dubious distinction of having been dismissed under both codes. One of Cardiff's recruits for their first season in the League, he joined from Llanelli RUFC after eight international appearances for Wales on the flank. He was selected for both Welsh International League matches since turning professional – against England and Australia.

Paul Rose

Born: December 20, 1952, Hull, Humberside, England.
Height: 6ft 2in.   *Weight:* 14st 10lb.
Position: Second row.
Club: Hull.
Great Britain Honours
Debut (full): July 1974 v Australia (in Sydney)
Appearances (full): two (three as sub).
Club Honours
Division One: winners 1978/79 (Hull KR)
Challenge Cup: winners 1979/80 (Hull KR); runners up 1982/83 (Hull)
Premiership Trophy: runners up 1982/83 (Hull)
Yorkshire Cup: winners 1974/75 (Hull KR) 1982/83, 1983/84 (Hull); runners up 1975/76, 1980/81 (both Hull KR)
BBC2 Floodlit Trophy: winners 1977/78 (Hull KR).

After ten years at Craven Park, Paul made the short journey across Hull in 1982 to the Boulevard. It proved a giant leap for his career. Not only did he appear in his second Challenge Cup final at Wembley before the season was out, he also regained his Great Britain place – four years after making his last appearance.

The second row forward burst onto the scene as a 17-year-old, helped Hull K.R. to a Yorkshire Cup victory and then spent a summer playing in Australia with Dapto to improve his game. He was a member of the Great Britain touring team in 1974 and would have made the squad in 1979 but for injury.

Following his £30,000 move to Hull in 1982, he was selected for the third Test against Australia at

Headingley in the November – four years after his last Great Britain appearance and eight years after his debut.

Paul's second Wembley appearance in 1983 ended ignominiously, when he became the first player to be sent to the 'sin bin' in a Challenge Cup final.

Lindsay Rotherforth

Born: 1964, Wakefield, West
    Yorkshire, England.
Height: 5ft 8in.   *Weight:* 11st 2lb.
Position: Winger.
Club: Wakefield Trinity.
Club Honours
Leading try scorer: 1982/83 season.

Lindsay, a summer signing from Redhill amateur in 1982, was Wakefield's top scorer in his first season with 18 tries. The club also won promotion to the First Division that year as runners up to Fulham, but Lindsay was mainly sidelined by injury.

Garry Schofield

Born: July 1, 1965, Leeds, West
    Yorkshire, England.
Height: 6ft 0in.   *Weight:* 13st 5lb.
Position: Centre.
Club: Hull.
Great Britain Honours
Debut (full): February 1984 v
    France (in Leeds)
    (under 24): November 1983 v
    France (in Villeneuve)
Appearances (full): one
    (under 24): two as sub.
Club Honours
Yorkshire Cup: winners 1983/84
League's leading try scorer: 1983/
    84.

Garry was the second youngest player to appear for Great Britain (a month older than Roger Millward), when he made his debut in the second Test with France at Headingley in February 1984.

He had captained Yorkshire and England schoolboys, as well as the BARLA Great Britain team, when he signed for Hull in September 1982, from Hunslet Parkside Amateur rugby league team. He played his first senior game in September 1983, scored a hat trick of tries against Leeds a month later and was picked for Great Britain's under 24 team in the November in one of the fastest rises on record. Garry's amazing first season, in which he broke the Hull post war try scoring record, was crowned when he gained selection for the 1984 summer tour. He enjoys squash, tennis, darts, cricket and table tennis – all of which he plays with the same determination as his rugby.

Glyn Shaw

Born: April 11, 1951, Neath, South
    Wales.
Height: 6ft 2in.   *Weight:* 15st 2lb.
Position: Prop forward.
Club: Wigan.
Great Britain Honours
Debut (full): November 1980 v New
    Zealand (in Bradford)
Appearances (full): one.
Club Honours
Division one: winners 1977/78
    (Widnes)
Challenge Cup: winners 1978/79,
    1980/81 (Widnes);
Premiership Trophy: winners 1979/
    80 (Widnes); runners up 1977/78
    (Widnes)

Glyn Shaw

John Player Trophy: winners 1978/79 (Widnes) 1982/83 (Wigan); runners up 1977/78, 1979/80 (both Widnes)

Lancashire Cup: winners 1978/79, 1979/80 (both Widnes).

Glyn joined Widnes in November 1977 after a very successful Rugby Union career with Neath, which included 12 Welsh caps.

By the end of his first professional season he had made his Welsh debut, appeared in the final of the John Player Trophy and Premiership Trophy, and been a member of the Championship winning team.

In 1980 he made his one and only appearance for Great Britain, against New Zealand at Odsal. It did not take Glyn long to start winning honours with his new club, Wigan, after a £30,000 transfer in November 1981. First came the surprise John Player Cup success over Leeds in 1983, and 12 months later, Wigan were at Wembley for the Challenge Cup final against Widnes, though unfortunately Glyn never made the final squad.

Trevor Skerrett

Born: March 6, 1954, Leeds, West Yorkshire, England.

Height: 5ft 11in.   *Weight:* 13st 13lb.

Position: Prop forward.

Club: Hull.

Great Britain Honours

Debut (full): June 1979 v Australia (in Brisbane)
   (under 24): November 1977 v France (in Hull)

Appearances (full): ten
   (under 24): one.

Club Honours

Division One: winners 1982/83 (Hull)

Challenge Cup: winners 1981/82

(Hull); runners up 1978/79
(Wakefield Trinity) 1982/83
(Hull)
Premiership Trophy: runners up
1980/81, 1981/82, 1982/83 (all
Hull)
John Player Trophy: winners 1981/
82 (Hull)
Yorkshire Cup: winners 1982/83,
1983/84 (both Hull); runners up
1974/75 (Wakefield Trinity)
Man of the Match Awards: 1981/82
John Player Trophy Final.

Equally as effective at prop or
second row, Trevor joined Wakefield
Trinity from Bison Sports in 1974.
He had made only six first team
appearances before he was appearing in the classic Yorkshire Cup
final of that year, which Wakefield

lost 16-13 to Hull KR. Eligible for
Wales through parentage, he made
six appearances for them and was
springboarded into the Great
Britain team for the 1979 tour of
Australia. He was made Great
Britain captain for the 1983/84
Tests against France, but had to
miss both through injury. He also
missed the 1984 tour, after being
selected as captain. Trevor left his
native West Riding in June 1980 to
join the progressive Hull outfit for a
then world record fee of £40,000. He
has appeared in all Hull's major
finals since, including the 1981/82
John Player Trophy final, when he
was made man of the match in a
stormy encounter with local rivals
Hull KR.

Trevor Skerrett

Andrew Smith

Born: December 17, 1958, Halifax,
  West Yorkshire, England.
Height: 5ft 11in. *Weight:* 12st 7lb.
Position: Winger.
Club: Leeds.
Club Honours
John Player Trophy: winners 1983/
  84; runners up 1982/83.

Andrew, a Yorkshire County Rugby
Union player, joined Leeds in March
1982 and scored on his debut
against Widnes a week later. He
notched five tries from eight outings
in that first term, and the following
season was a regular member. He
scored 11 tries, including a hat trick
in the John Player Trophy match
against York as Leeds went on to
the final. Andrew's father Brian was
a winger with York and then, as
coach, steered Huddersfield to the
Second Division championship in
1974/75

Gary Smith

Born: April 21, 1954, York, North
  Yorkshire, England.
Height: 5ft 7in. *Weight:* 13st 0lb.
Position: Loose forward.
Club: York.
Club Honours
Division two: winners 1980/81
Yorkshire Cup: runners up 1978/79.

Gary joined York in 1971, and spent
most of his career playing as a
utility back. But a recent switch to
loose forward has revitalised his
game and he gave an outstanding
display as York narrowly lost to
First Division Wigan in the 1984
Challenge Cup semi final.
   Gary threatened to become a
great player and perhaps a move
away from York would have aided

his career, but he remained loyal to
them. He scored York's only try in
their 18-8 Yorkshire Cup final
defeat by Bradford Northern in 1978
– his one major cup final
appearance.

Gordon Smith

Gordon Smith

Born: 1956, Greymouth, New
  Zealand.
Height: 5ft 6in. *Weight:* 11st 7lb.
Position: Scrum half.
Club: Hull Kingston Rovers.
New Zealand Honours
Debut (full): 1979 v Great Britain
Appearances (full): 14.
Club Honours
Division one: winners 1983/84.

Another of Hull Kingston Rovers'
New Zealanders, Gordon joined
them from West Coast in October
1982, and readily slotted in at scrum
half.
   He has more than 50 points to his
credit in Test matches and has
kicked 24 goals. In all games for
New Zealand, he has kicked 60
goals and scored 135 points. He was
West Coast Sportsman of the Year
for 1983.

Mike Smith

Mike Smith

Born: January 26, 1958, Hull,
  Humberside, England.
Height: 6ft 0in.   *Weight:* 13st 6lb.
Position: Centre.
Club: Hull Kingston Rovers.
Great Britain Honours
Debut (full): July 1979 v New
  Zealand (Auckland)
  (under 24): November 1976 v
  France (Hull)
Appearances (full): nine (one as sub)
  (under 24): seven.
Club Honours
Division One: winners 1978/79,
  1983/84
Challenge Cup: winners 1979/80;
  runners up 1980/81
Premiership Trophy: winners 1980/
  81, 1983/84
John Player Trophy: runners up
  1981/82
Yorkshire Cup: runners up 1980/81
BBC2 Floodlit Trophy: winners
  1977/78; runners up 1979/80.

Mike started playing rugby at eight
and went on to represent England
schoolboys at under 16 level.

He joined Hull Kingston Rovers
as a 17-year-old and two years later
gave an outstanding performance in
the Floodlit final against St. Helens.
His try and brilliant all round play
helped destroy the opposition to give
Mike his first senior honour in the
game.

He made his Great Britain under
24 debut against France at his home
ground in 1976, and in 1979 made
his full Great Britain bow on the
Australasia tour, scoring a try in
the match against New Zealand at
Auckland. He has made ten Great
Britain appearances, the last as substitute against France in the second
Test at Leeds in 1984.

Some critics believe he has yet to
reproduce his excellent club form at
international level. He had the
chance to prove the critics wrong as
a member of the 1984 Great Britain
touring team.

Peter Smith

Born: September 17, 1955,
  Featherstone, West Yorkshire,
  England.
Height: 6ft 1in   *Weight:* 14st 9lb.
Position: Second row/loose forward.
Club: Featherstone Rovers.
Great Britain Honours
Debut (full): June 1977 v Australia
  (in Brisbane – World Cup)
  (under 24): October 1978 v
  Australia (in Hull)
Appearances (full): one (five as sub)
  (under 24): one.
Club Honours
Division One: winners 1976/77
Division Two: winners 1979/80
Challenge Cup: winners 1982/83
Yorkshire Cup: runners up 1976/77,

1977/78.

Peter, a product of the junior team at Featherstone, has been one of the club's top try scoring forwards in post war years.

His attacking style of play earned him selection for the Great Britain

Peter Smith

squad for the 1977 World Cup and he went on to make six appearances for the senior side. His last was the most surprising. He had not played for Featherstone during the 1983/84 season because of a back injury, but was selected as substitute for the second Test with France at Headingley.

Ronnie Smith

Born: April 14, 1960, Liverpool,
  Merseyside, England.
Height: 5ft 11in.   *Weight:* 14st 0lb.
Position: Centre.
Club: Salford.
Great Britain Honours
Debut (under 24): January 1983 v
  France (in Carpentras)
Appearances (under 24): one as sub.
Club Honours

Promotion from Division Two 1982/
  83 season
Club leading goal scorer: 1982/83,
  1983/84.

A fast centre or second row forward, Ronnie showed his potential during his first full season in 1982/83. He finished with 197 points, 23 of them coming in one game against Huyton when he scored three tries and kicked seven goals.

His all-round ability earned him under 24 selection against France in January 1983 at Carpentras and he came on as substitute for Warrington's John Fieldhouse.

A former Lancashire schools and colts player, Ronnie joined Salford from the crack Wigan amateur side, St. Patricks.

He has a keen interest in show dogs.

Graham Steadman

Born: December 8, 1961, Castleford,
  West Yorkshire, England.
Height: 5ft 10in.   *Weight:* 12st 0lb.
Position: Stand off.
Club: York.
Club Honours
Challenge Cup: semi finalists 1983/
  84 Leading club try scorer: 1983/
  84.

Like so many York players in the 1983/84 season, Graham was motivated by the club's Challenge Cup run, which took them to the semi-finals. That glorious journey was ended by Wigan, but Graham maintained the form he had shown in the second half of the season. Two weeks after the Cup defeat, Graham broke the club scoring record for the most number of points in one game, with 24, including three tries in the

50-6 routing of Carlisle. His tally beat the previous record by two points. Remarkably, in his next game, he equalled that record of 24. Graham signed from Castleford Amateur Rugby League side, Sailors Home, in March 1982, scoring one try and kicking four goals in his five games before the end of that season.

In 1982/83, he showed his exciting potential. Despite playing only 16 games, he scored nine tries and kicked 12 goals. He is now rated in the £60,000 class. During the campaign his 11 goals in the match with Carlisle, and his 27 points in the same match, were both club records.

Gary Stephens

Born: August 23, 1952, Castleford, West Yorkshire, England.
Height: 5ft 5in.   *Weight:* 11st 0lb.
Position: Scrum half.
Club: Wigan.
Great Britain Honours
Debut (full): June 1979 v Australia (in Brisbane)
Appearances (full): five.
Club Honours
Challenge Cup: runners up 1983/84 (Wigan)
John Player Trophy: winners 1976/77 (Castleford)
Yorkshire Cup: winners 1977/78 (Castleford); runners up 1968/69, 1971/72 (both Castleford)
BBC Floodlit Trophy: winners 1976/77 (Castleford)
Man of the Match Awards: 1976/77 John Player Trophy Final.

After 15 years in the professional game, it looked as though Gary would be calling it a day during the 1983/84 season, when he lost his place in the Wigan side to 17-year-

Gary Stephens

old Keith Holden. But Gary battled back to regain his place in the team that eventually reached the Challenge Cup final at Wembley, although he had to survive a scrape with the disciplinary committee nine days before the Wembley date.

Gary's early playing days were spent with the Castleford Boys' team. He worked his way through the junior sides before joining his home town team as a professional in 1969.

Of all the honours he won with Castleford, the most cherished was his Man of the Match award in the 1976/77 John Player Trophy final. His excellent try played its part in Castleford's victory over Blackpool and paved the way for Gary to take the award, jointly with Borough's Howard Allen. He was top player in the 1976 Sydney Grade Grand

Final, playing for Manly-Warringah during one of the two seasons he spent in Australia.

A member of the England shadow squad for the 1975 World Championship, he eventually made his England debut in 1979, and that summer toured Australasia with the Great Britain squad. His debut came in the first test with Australia in Brisbane. Wigan paid £35,000 for Gary in November 1980, and his experience has played a big part in Alex Murphy's rebuilding programme at Central Park. Gary spent a short period on loan to nearby Warrington in 1983.

Publican Gary is an all-round sports enthusiast, and this stems from his schooldays when he represented Castleford schools at cricket, soccer, athletics, cross country and swimming.

David Stephenson

Born: December 3, 1958, Lytham St
Annes, Lancashire, England.
Height: 6ft 0in. *Weight:* 13st 4lb.
Position: Centre.
Club: Wigan.
Great Britain Honours
Debut (full): November 1982 v
Australia (in Wigan)
(under 24): November 1979 v
France (in Leigh)
Appearances (full): two
(under 24): five
Club Honours
Challenge Cup: runners up 1983/84
(Wigan)
John Player Trophy: winners 1982/
83 (Wigan)

An England schoolboy Rugby Union representative at under 15, 16 and 19 levels, David joined Salford in 1978 from Fylde RU Club. Recog-

nised as a fine centre, he made the first of his five appearances for the Great Britain Under 24 team at Leigh during his spell with Salford. But it was not until after his £60,000 move to Wigan in February 1982 that he gained his first full cap, and also his first honours at club level.

Nine months after his move to Wigan, he made his senior international debut against those awesome 1982 Kangaroos at Central Park. His first domestic honour came in the John Player final in January, 1983, when he was a member of the Wigan side that surprised Leeds with a 15-4 victory.

David enjoys reading, music, walking and sport in general. Due to a clerical error in January 1983 he was called up to play for the Rugby Union squad. A firm favourite at Central Park, David nearly did not become a Wigan player at all. Salford were offered £40,000 plus the £45,000 rated Phil Hogan from Hull KR for him. But, fortunately for Wigan, Salford refused the offer.

Nigel Stephenson

Born: October 12, 1950, Dewsbury,
West Yorkshire, England.
Height: 5ft 10in. *Weight:* 13st 8lb.
Position: Stand off.
Club: Wakefield Trinity.
Club Honours
Division One: winners 1979/80,
1980/81 (both Bradford Northern)
Premiership Trophy: runners up
1979/80 (Bradford Northern)
John Player Trophy: winners 1979/
80 (Bradford Northern)
Championship Play Off: winners
1972/73 (Dewsbury)
BBC Floodlit Trophy: runners up
1975/76 (Dewsbury).

As Nigel's career reaches the twilight, time it looks as though he will not now fulfil his ambition of playing at Wembley. He has come within one match three times, losing in the semi final with Dewsbury in 1973 and 1974 and with Bradford in 1979. Nigel joined Dewsbury as a 16-year-old in 1967, and between 1969 and 1972 played 103 consecutive games for the club. In 1972/73 he established the current Dewsbury record for most goals in a season (145) and most points (368). One of his most memorable matches was the 1973 Championship Play-off. Dewsbury had finished only eighth in the table and surprised everyone by reaching the final against third placed Leeds. Nigel scored one try and kicked five goals in an amazing 22-13 victory. Nigel moved across Yorkshire to Bradford in 1978 and collected two First Division championship medals and a John Player Trophy winners' medal. A £20,000 deal took him to the newly-formed Carlisle team in July 1981 and helped them to first season promotion. Nigel did not stay to taste First Division football. Instead, he moved to Wakefield for another £20,000 to become their record signing – and for the second successive season gained promotion. As Wakefield languished near the bottom of the First Division in 1984, Nigel was one of several senior players asked to stand down in March for the rest of the season to make way for up and coming juniors.

Charlie Stone

Born: September 12, 1950, Pontefract, West Yorkshire, England.

Height: 6ft 0in.   *Weight:* 14st 0lb.
Position: Prop forward.
Club: Featherstone Rovers.
England Honours
Debut: November 1975 v Australia (in Leeds)
Appearances: one.
Club Honours
First Division: winners 1976/77 (Featherstone Rovers) 1982/83 (Hull)
Second Division: winners 1978/79 (Hull)
Challenge Cup: winners 1972/73 (Featherstone Rovers) 1981/82 (Hull); runners up 1973/74 (Featherstone Rovers) 1979/80, 1982/83 (both Hull)
Premiership Trophy: runners up 1980/81, 1981/82, 1982/83 (all Hull)
John Player Trophy: winners 1981/82 (Hull)
Yorkshire Cup: winners 1982/83 (Hull); runners up 1976/77, 1977/78 (Featherstone Rovers)
BBC2 Floodlit Trophy: winners 1979/80 (Hull)
Captain Morgan Trophy: runners up 1973/74 (Featherstone Rovers).

Charlie returned to his first club Featherstone Rovers, for the 1983/84 season 13 years after initially joining them from Pontefract Rugby Union club. Charlie made only one international appearance for England in the post World Cup match against Australia at Leeds in 1975. He was a member of the 1979 Great Britain tour party, but never played in a Test.

At club level, however, it has been success all the way. His first major honours came in the 1973 Challenge Cup final at Wembley – the first of his five Wembley appearances – when Featherstone beat Bradford

Northern by 33 points to 14 in the highest scoring Wembley final ever. The First Divison title followed in 1976/77 before Second Division Hull came in with a bid of £15,000 for him in 1978. Hull were promoted as Second Division champions that first season and Charlie went on to make three Challenge Cup final appearances with them.

His last Wembley appearance in the 1983 final was against Featherstone and it was ironic that he was the Hull player penalised to give Steve Quinn his match winning penalty kick in the final minute.

Clive Sullivan

Born: April 9, 1943, Cardiff, South Wales.
Height: 5ft 11in.   *Weight:* 12st 7lb.
Position: Coach.
Club: Unattached.
Great Britain Honours
Debut (full): January 1967 v France (in Carcassonne)
Appearances (full): 17.
Club Honours
Division one: winners 1978/79 (Hull KR)
Challenge Cup: winners 1979/80 (Hull KR)
Yorkshire Cup: winners 1969/70 (Hull) 1974/75 (Hull KR); runners up 1975/76 (Hull KR)
BBC Floodlit Trophy: winners 1977/78 (Hull KR); runners up 1979/80 (Hull KR).

Born and bred in Cardiff, Clive has been adopted by Hull after playing Rugby League in the city for over 20 years. He appeared for both Humberside clubs and to show complete impartiality scored more than 100 tries for each.

A fast and versatile winger – who could also play at full back - Clive had won most of the game's honours by the time he was reaching retirement age in 1980: all except a Challenge Cup winners' medal. That situation was rectified in the 1980 final as Clive and Hull KR defeated their Humberside neighbours in an emotional final. At the age of 37, Clive had his winners' medal at last. Clive had joined Hull in 1961 and stayed there 13 years before moving to Rovers. He had a 12 month loan spell with Oldham in 1980, before returning to Hull in 1981 for £20,000. But the glory days were over and the former steelworker took charge of the League's bottom club, Doncaster, tasting defeat for the first time in his long career.

Clive appeared on the TV programme, This Is Your life in 1972 shortly after he led Great Britain to victory in that year's World Cup. He played 17 times for Great Britain and his loyalty to club and country was rewarded with the M.B.E. in 1974. Doncaster and Clive parted company in the 1984 close season.

Graham Swale

Born: January 3, 1958, Workington, Cumbria, England.
Height: 5ft 8in.   *Weight:* 14st 0lb.
Position: Loose forward.
Club: Batley.
Club Honours
Club Top goalscorer: 1980/81 (Huddersfield), 1981/82 (Bramley).

Practical joker Graham Swale may not leave the game with a lot of trophies . . . but there will certainly be a lot of memories. Such as the incident in October 1981, when, following Hudderfield's game with Huyton he nipped into the Huyton dressing room and stole coach Geoff Fletcher's hair piece. The prank got Graham banned at Huddersfield for six months, but the suspension was never enforced, because 11 days later he signed for Bramley.

His last season at Huddersfield had been one of his best. He was top goalscorer with 65 – eight of them coming in the game against Huyton. His move to Bramley was followed by another to Halifax in January 1983 and a third to Batley a few months later.

Eddie Syzmala

Born: June 24, 1954, Barrow-in-
    Furness, Cumbria, England.
Height: 5ft 10in.   *Weight:* 12st 0lb.
Position: Hooker.
Club: Barrow.
Great Britain Honours
Debut (full): December 1981 v
    France (in Hull)
    (under 24): November 1976 v
    France (in Hull)
Appearances (full): one (one as sub)
    (under 24): two.
Club Honours
Division Two: winners 1983/84.
Lancashire Cup: winners 1983/84
    John Player Cup: runners up
    1980/81.

A tough competitive hooker, Eddie made 15 appearances before the Rugby League disciplinary committee, between 1975 and 1981. He is proud of his tattooed torso and muscles built through pumping weights. He made his Great Britain under 24 debut against France at Hull in 1976 and his first senior England international appearance followed in 1979, when he went on as sub-

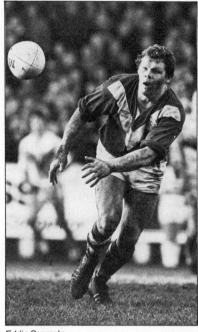

Eddie Syzmala

stitute for Phil Hogan against France.

Two years later came his full Great Britain debut, when again he went on as substitute in the game against France at Hull. He was a member of the Barrow side which lost to Warrington in the final of the John Player Cup in 1980/81, a disappointment overcome in 1984 when he helped Barrow, the Second Division underdogs, to beat mighty Widnes in the Lancashire Cup final.

Howie Tamati

Born: January 3, 1955, Whaitara,
    New Zealand.
Height: 6ft 0lb.   *Weight:* 12st 8lb.
Position: Hooker.

Club: Wigan.
New Zealand Honours
Debut (full): 1979 v Great Britain
Appearances (full): 16.
Club Honours
Challenge Cup: runners up 1983/84.

Howie underwent a series of foot
tendon operations at the start of
1983, yet in May that year he was
back in action for Central Districts
in Australia's K.B. Cup. One of his
greatest performances came in the
second Test with Australia at Brisbane. The Kiwis brought off one of
the biggest shocks in their history
by defeating the Kangaroos and
Howie played a monumental role,
being involved in 37 tackles in a
non- stop performance. In October
1983 he was made captain of his
country for the game against Papua
New Guinea and led them to a
record 60-20 win. He has made 34
New Zealand appearances – 16 in
Tests – and has scored five tries.

He joined Wigan from Taranaki
for the 1983/84 season and ended
the season playing for them in the
Challenge Cup against Widnes at
Wembley. His cousin Kevin was on
the opposing side.

Howie Tamati

Kevin Tamati

Born: September 2, 1954, Hastings, New Zealand.
Height: 5ft 10in.   *Weight:* 15st 0lb.
Position: Prop forward/second row.
Club: Widnes.
New Zealand Honours
Debut (full): 1979 v Great Britain
Appearances (full): 14.
Club Honours
Challenge Cup: winners 1983/84
    John Player Special Trophy:
    runners up 1983/84
Lancashire Cup: runners up 1983/
    84.

Kiwi international Kevin joined Widnes in October 1982 from Randwick and impressed so much that he was asked back for a second term in 1983.

He appeared in the final of both the Lancashire Cup and John Player Special Trophy that season but, surprisingly for Widnes, they lost both. He gained compensation in fine style when Widnes won the 1984 Challenge Cup final at Wembley . . . especially as his cousin Howie was on the opposing Wigan side. It was Kevin who won the battle of the Tamatis, giving a performance that earned him the runners up slot for the Lance Todd award.

Steve Tickle

Born: April 12, 1954, St. Helens, Merseyside, England.
Height: 5ft 10in.   *Weight:* 12st 0lb.
Position: Full back.
Club: Barrow.
Club Honours
Division Two: winners 1983/84
Lancashire Cup: winners 1983/84.

The St. Helens school teacher is a product of the famous academy, Cowley School, where he was coached by Ray French.

He joined Barrow in 1978 from Waterloo Rugby Union club and succeeded former Waterloo club mate Ian Ball as Barrow's goal kicker for the 1982/83 season. He landed 70 goals and 144 points to make him the club's leading scorer. Nine of those 70 goals came in the 57-0 hammering of Halifax in a First Division game. The 1983/84 Lancashire Cup win against Widnes was the highlight of his career, for it was his 51st minute drop goal that helped Barrow to their first trophy success for 29 years.

Steve put himself into the Barrow record books in 1984, when he scored 28 points in the 80-8 humiliation of Kent Invicta.

David Topliss

Born: December 29, 1949, Wakefield, West Yorkshire, England.
Height: 5ft 8in.   *Weight:* 11st 2lb.
Position: Stand off.
Club: Hull.
Great Britain Honours
Debut (full): November 1973 v
    Australia (at Wembley)
Appearances (full): four.
Club Honours
Division One: winners 1982/83
    (Hull)
Challenge Cup: winners 1981/82
    (Hull); runners up: 1978/79
    (Wakefield Trinity) 1982/83
    (Hull)
Premiership Trophy: runners up
    1981/82, 1982/83 (Hull)
John Player Trophy: runners up
    1971/72 (Wakefield Trinity)
Yorkshire Cup: winners 1982/83,
    1983/84 (both Hull); runners up
    1974/75 (Wakefield Trinity)

Man of the Match Awards: Lance Todd award 1978/79 Challenge Cup final.

David moved to Hull after 13 years at Wakefield Trinity for the start of the 1980/81 season and proceded to lead them to six major finals. He joined Wakefield in 1968 from local amateur side Normanton and became an outstanding captain ... never more so than when Wakefield took on Widnes in the 1979 Challenge Cup final.

Although Wakefield lost, David took the Lance Todd award – the last player from a losing side to lift the trophy. David's international career spanned nine years from November 1973, yet he gained only four caps. An attacking player with great flair, David took his skills to Australia in the mid-seventies to play with Penrith. In 1981 he joined Hull, a move which revived his fortunes in spectacular fashion. He captained the 'Airlie Birds' to consecutive Challenge Cup finals, two Premiership Trophy finals and two Yorkshire Cups.

A prolific try scorer with more than 200 to his credit, he has figured in the top ten list five times. His best placing was in 1972/73 when he was fourth.

Sammy Turnbull

Born: September 14, 1954, Salford, Greater Manchester, England.
Height: 6ft 0in. *Weight:* 12st 0lb.
Position: Second row forward/prop forward/centre.
Club: Salford.
Great Britain Honours
Debut (under 24): November 1976 v France (in Hull)
Appearances (under 24): two.

Club Honours
Division One: winners 1975/76
Premiership Trophy: runners up 1975/76
Lancashire Cup: runners up 1975/76.

A powerful all-round player, Sammy shared Salford's glory season of 1975/76 when they won the First Division Championship and reached the final of both the Lancashire Cup and Premiership Trophy.

Following that successful season, he was selected for the Great Britain under 24 side against France in 1976. He scored a try and was selected for a second match with France, but has never played international rugby since, partly because of a serious knee injury, which at one time threatened his career.

Norman Turley

Born: September 5, 1955, Leigh, Greater Manchester, England.
Height: 6ft 3in. *Weight:* 15st 2lb.
Position: Loose forward.
Club: Blackpool Borough.
Club Honours
Club leading points scorer: 1980/81 (Rochdale Hornets), 1983/84 (Blackpool Borough).

Drop goal specialist Norman landed 18 in the 1978/79 season – a record until broken in 1980/81 by Whitehaven's Arnie Walker. Norman started his career at Blackpool before moving to Rochdale Hornets. He had a loan spell at Swinton between November 1981 and February 1982 and returned to Borough for the 1983/84 season. His boot has been instrumental in their revival and a push for a place in the top

Division for the first time in four years. His goalkicking put him in the Borough record books during the latest campaign. His 11 goals in the match with Carlisle, and the 27 points in the same match were club records.

David Ward

Born: December 16, 1953, Morley, West Yorkshire, England.
Height: 5ft 10in.   *Weight:* 14st 0lb.
Position: Hooker.
Club: Leeds.
Great Britain Honours
Debut (full): June 1977 v France (in Auckland – World Cup)
   (under 24): November 1976 v France (in Hull)
Appearances (full): 12
   (under 24): two as sub.
Club Honours
Challenge Cup: winners 1976/77, 1977/78
Premiership Trophy: winners 1974/ 75, 1978/79; runners up 1983/84
John Player Trophy: winners 1972/ 73, 1983/84; runners up 1982/83
Yorkshire Cup: winners 1972/73, 1973/74, 1976/77, 1979/80, 1980/ 81
Championship Play-off: winners 1971/72; runners up 1972/73
Awards: Trumanns Man of Steel – 1977, Trumanns Man of Steel Young Player of the Year – 1977.

David, one of the outstanding club captains of recent years, led Leeds to Challenge Cup triumph in successive years in 1977 and 1978. David himself kicked the drop goal two minutes from time which clinched a 14-12 victory over St. Helens. David's senior career has all been spent at Leeds whom he joined from Shaw Cross Boys Club as a 17-year-

old in May 1971. By then he had already gained representative honours with Yorkshire under 15's and under 17's and toured France with England schools under 15's.

He has appeared in a major Cup final with Leeds every season since 1971/72 apart from two – 1975/76 and 1981/82. David has made two Great Britain tours, and 12 appearances for the senior team since his debut in the 1977 World Cup match with France in Auckland.

He was awarded the first Trumanns Man of Steel trophy in 1977, along with their Young Player of the Year title – the first person to have won both awards in the same season.

Kevin Ward

Born: August 5, 1957, Wakefield, West Yorkshire, England.
Height: 6ft 1in.   *Weight:* 14st 12lb.
Position: Prop forward.
Club: Castleford.
Great Britain Honours
Debut (full): February 1984 v France (in Leeds)
   (under 24): January 1980 v France (in Carcassonne)
Appearances (full): one
   (under 24): three.
Club Honours
Premiership Trophy: runners up 1983/84.
Yorkshire Cup: winners 1981/82.

Kevin was a relative late comer to the senior game preferring amateur soccer before he joined Castleford in November 1978 at the age of 21. But it was not long before he had established himself and he was selected for Great Britain under 24's 12 months after going to Wheldon Road.

His big break came in February 1984, when he was drafted into the Great Britain senior side for the second Test against France at Headingley, in place of the injured Len Casey.

David Watkins

Born: March 5, 1942, Blaina, Gwent, South Wales.
Height: 5ft 6in.   *Weight:* 11st 6lb.
Position: Coach/Managing Director.
Club: Cardiff City.
Great Britain Honours
Debut (full): March 1971 v France (in St. Helens)
Appearances (full): two (four as sub).
Club Honours
Division One: winners 1973/74, 1975/76 (both Salford)
Challenge Cup: runners up 1968/69 (Salford)
Premiership Trophy: runners up 1975/76 (Salford)
John Player Trophy: runners up 1972/73 (Salford)
Lancashire Cup: winner 1972/73 (Salford); runners up 1973/74, 1975/76 (both Salford)
BBC Floodlit Trophy: winners 1974/75 (Salford).

After his wonderful career in Rugby Union, it was hard to imagine David could emulate that success in the professional game — but he did.

The mercurial British Lion's and Newport Stand off played for Wales 21 times, before joining Salford in 1967 for a £14,000 signing on fee. He adapted well to the new code and, in 1971, was selected for Great Britain appearing as substitute against France at St. Helens. He became a dual Welsh

international in 1975 and went on to play the 13-a-side code for his country 14 times, including the 1975 World Championships.

In the 1972/73 season he was the League's top goalkicker with a world record 221. In the process he kicked 13 in one game against Keighley to equal the club's 32-year-old record. David scored in all Salford's matches that season, a feat he repeated in the next campaign to make him the first to have done so in two seasons. Between August 1972 and April 1974 he played 92 matches for his club, kicked 403 goals and scored 41 tries to give him a total of 929 points. He was coach of the Great Britain team for the 1977 World Cup, before moving on shortly afterwards to Swinton. He was appointed managing director of the newly-formed Cardiff City club in 1981, and in December of that year took over as coach from John Mantle.

David Watkinson

Born: November 19, 1954, York, North Yorkshire, England.
Height: 5ft 9in.   *Weight:* 13st 13lb.
Position: Hooker.
Club: Hull Kingston Rovers.
Great Britain Honours
Debut (full): June 1979 v Australia (in Sydney)
Appearances (full): three (one as sub).
Club Honours
Division One: winners 1978/79, 1983/84
Challenge Cup: winners 1979/80; runners up 1980/81
Premiership Trophy: winners 1980/81
John Player Trophy: runners up 1981/82

David Watkinson

France in Avignon. But after just two minutes of the game David broke his leg when he fell awkwardly while fielding a loose ball.

Terry Webb

Born: April 3, 1960, Brisbane, Australia.
Height: 5ft 10in.   *Weight:* 13st 7lb.
Position: Loose forward.
Club: Leeds.
Club Honours
John Player Special Trophy: winners 1983/84.

One of several Australians to join Leeds for the 1983/84 season, Terry flew in from the Redcliffe club in Brisbane.

The aggressive loose forward scored his first points with a try during the 44-10 victory over Fulham. His first British honours followed as Leeds defeated Widnes in the final of the 1984 John Player Special Trophy at Central Park, Wigan. Terry signed a new contract in April 1984, which will keep him at Leeds for a further three seasons.

BBC2 Floodlit Trophy: winners 1977/78.

A product of the highly successful Heworth Amateur side in York, David had trials with his home town team and Wakefield Trinity before signing for Hull Kingston Rovers in January 1977. He plays as hooker, but can capably cover as a prop. One of his best performances was in Rovers' Floodlit final win over St. Helens in the 1977/78 season. David was a surprise choice for the Great Britain tour of Australasia in 1979 and played in the second Test coming on as substitute against Australia in Sydney. He was recalled to the international arena in 1984 for the first Test with

Graeme West

Born: December 5, 1954, Hawera, New Zealand.
Height: 6ft 5in.   *Weight:* 15st 10lb.
Position: Second row forward.
Club: Wigan
New Zealand Honours
Debut (full): 1975 v Australia
Appearances (full): 17.
Club Honours
Challenge Cup: runners up 1983/84
John Player Trophy: winners 1982/83.

New Zealand captain Graeme West signed a five year contract at Wigan

Graeme West

off a surprising 19-12 win in Brisbane. Graeme scored one of the Kiwi's tries.

Colin Whitfield

Born: September 29, 1960, Widnes,
   Cheshire, England.
Height: 5ft 11in.   *Weight:* 13st 0lb.
Position: Centre. Clubs: Wigan.
Great Britain Honours
Debut (under 24): January 1981 v
   France (in Villeneuve)
Appearances (under 24): one.

Club Honours
Challenge Cup: runners up 1983/84
   (Wigan)
John Player Trophy: winners 1982/
   83 (Wigan).

Colin Whitfield was a major factor in Wigan's run to the 1984 Cup final at Wembley. He scored two tries and kicked 15 goals during the club's drive to glory, including three goals and a try in the semi final which put paid to the hopes of Second Division York.

He joined Wigan in a £65,000 deal that took Trevor Stockley and ex-Bolton Wanderers footballer Roy Heaney to Salford in November 1981. In the three seasons he has been at Central Park, Colin has been leading goalscorer. His 104 goals in 1982/83 made him eighth in the League list, and again the following season he finished in the top ten, having scored another ton'. Walking out at Wembley in the 1984 Challenge Cup final was Colin's proudest moment in the game. But not far behind will be his captaining of the Wigan side to victory over Leeds in the 1983 John Player Trophy final.

The one surprising thing about

in November 1982, after joining them from Taranaki. Coach Alex Murphy declared West the best second row forward in the world.

He had been leading New Zealand try scorer in 1979 with 13 from appearances with Taranaki and Central Districts and was New Zealand Player of the Year in 1981. He once scored six tries in a game, for Taranaki against Central Districts.

He flew 12,000 miles from England to take part in the first Test with Australia in New Zealand in June 1983, only to find himself on the substitutes bench. Disgusted, he announced he was going home. He was persuaded to change his mind and appointed captain for the second Test in which New Zealand brought

Colin Whitfield

Colin's career to date, is that he has made only one under 24 appearance – in which he kicked three goals. Surely, senior honours must be just around the corner for this popular Central Park player.

Fred Whitfield

Born: April 20, 1958, Widnes, Cheshire, England.
Height: 6ft 1in.　*Weight:* 15st 0lb.
Position: Second row/prop.
Club: Widnes.
Club Honours
Challenge Cup: winners 1983/84
Premiership Trophy: winners 1981/ 82, 1982/83
John Player Special Trophy:

runners up 1983/84
Lancashire Cup: runners up 1983/84.

A talented player who came through the junior ranks at Widnes, Fred has so far had limited experience with the first team. He made his debut in 1980 and has since played in two Premiership Trophy winning finals.

In 1982 he came on as substitute in the victory over Hull, and the following year – in a repeat success – he wore the number 11 shirt before himself being substituted by Steve O'Neill. With plenty of time on his side, Fred can look forward to a lengthy and successful career. He was chosen for the initial Great Britain training squad for the 1984 summer tour.

Ronnie Wileman

Born: December 19, 1954, Barnsley, South Yorkshire, England.
Height: 5ft 8in.　*Weight:* 12st 4lb.
Position: Hooker.
Club: Hull
Club Honours
Challenge Cup: winners 1981/82 (Hull); runners up 1979/80 (Hull)
Premiership Trophy: runners up 1980/81, 1981/82 (both Hull)
John Player Trophy: winners 1981/ 82 (Hull)
Yorkshire Cup: runners up 1978/79 (York)
BBC Floodlit Trophy: winners 1979/ 80 (Hull).

Barnsley-based Ronnie moved from York to Hull for £20,000 at the start of the 1979/80 season. He was soon playing in the winning BBC Floodlit Trophy team to earn his first honour in the game as Hull beat deadly rivals Hull KR in the last Floodlit

124

final. That season Ronnie scored a match winning try in the Challenge Cup semi final against Widnes to book a first Wembley appearance. But he ended up on the losing side against Hull KR.

In 1982 Ronnie scored the only try of the John Player Trophy final in which Hull beat Hull KR 12-4, and he made a second Wembley appearance. Hull and Widnes produced the first drawn Cup Final since 1954. Ronnie was injured and missed the replay, which Hull won 18-9 at Elland Road. Ronnie has not been a regular in the Hull side since then and in March 1984 he joined Doncaster on loan, teaming up with his old colleague Clive Sullivan.

The move started disastrously – Ronnie was sent off twice within four days at the beginning of April. These dismissals earned him a 16 match suspension.

Alf Wilkinson

Born: April 15, 1954, Leigh, Greater
  Manchester, England.
Height: 6ft 1in.   *Weight:* 16st 0lb.
Position: Prop forward.
Club: Leigh.
Great Britain Honours
Debut (under 24): December 1977 v
  France (in Tonneins)
Appearances (under 24): one.
Club Honours
Division One: winners 1981/82
Division Two: winners 1977/78
Lancashire Cup: winner 1981/82.

Once tipped as a potential Great Britain prop, Alf has never lived up to that high expectation, but he is nevertheless one of the most consistent practitioners of the open side prop art. His career has been interrupted by injuries and his loyalty to the Leigh club has been rewarded with a testimonial.

Ian Wilkinson

Born: September 3, 1960,
  Hemsworth, West Yorkshire,
  England.
Height: 6ft 0in.   *Weight:* 15st 0lb.
Position: Centre/full back.
Club: Leeds.
Club Honours
John Player Special Trophy:
  winners 1983/84; runners up
  1982/83.

The former Scunthorpe United soccer player joined Leeds from amateur side Hemsworth Miners Welfare in March 1980. He established himself as a regular first team player during 1982/83, when he was the club's top try scorer with 16. In the game with Workington in January, he scored the first hat trick of his senior career. He was on the losing side in the 1982/83 John Player final, when Leeds went down to underdogs Wigan. A year later when Leeds and Widnes met in the final, Leeds were the underdogs – and Ian ended up with a winners' medal. He took his first step towards international football when he was selected for the Australian and New Zealand tour squad early in 1984, although he did not make the trip.

Brynmor Williams

Born: October 29, 1952, Cardigan,
  Wales.
Height: 5ft 10in.   *Weight:* 13st 8lb.
Position: Scrum half.
Club: Cardiff City.
Welsh Honours
Debut: October 1982 v Australia (in
  Cardiff) Appearances: one.

Brynmor resisted the urge to make the switch to Rugby League in Cardiff's first season in 1981/82. But a £15,000 offer persuaded him to change his mind the following season and leave behind a highly successful ten year Rugby Union career. His amateur days saw him play for Cardiff, Newport, and Swansea at club level – and for the Barbarians, Wales and the British Lions. Three months after his first pro game for Cardiff he was donning a Welsh Rugby League shirt for the international against Australia at Cardiff, and scoring Wales' only try in the 37-7 defeat.

A Building Society Branch Manager, Brynmor had a fine record as a junior athlete in sprint's and the high jump. He won silver medals in both the British Youths and Schools Championships.

John Wood

Born: April 1, 1956, Widnes, Cheshire.
Height: 6ft 1in.   *Weight:* 16st 2lb.
Position: Prop forward.
Club: Widnes.
Great Britain Honours
Debut (under 24): November 1976 v France (in Hull)
Appearances (under 24): two.
Club Honours
Division One: winners 1977/78 (Widnes)
Challenge Cup: runners up 1975/76 (Widnes)
John Player Trophy: winners 1975/76 (Widnes)

John was an under 18 England international at Rugby Union. He had a trial with Widnes at 16, but refused to commit himself to League until he was 19 when he joined them

from Widnes RUFC. He was in the team which won the John Player Trophy and lost the Challenge Cup final in 1976 before moving to Wigan. He joined league newcomers Fulham in 1980 and played 25 games in their promotion year. After two seasons with the Londoners he moved back north to Salford for the 1983/84 season. His stay at the Willows lasted less than six months, then he was back with Widnes in a £30,000 deal, which took Eric Prescott and John Taylor the other way.

A member of the initial Great Britain squad for the 1984 summer tour down under, he pulled out before the final squad was announced because of family commitments.

John Woods

Born: September 14, 1956, Leigh, Greater Manchester, England.
Height: 5ft 11in.   *Weight:* 11st 10lb.
Position: Player/coach.
Club: Leigh.
Great Britain Honours
Debut (full): June 1979 v Australia (in Brisbane)
  (under 24): November 1977 v France (in Hull)
Appearances (full): seven (three as sub)
  (under 24): five.
Club Honours
Division One: winners 1981/82
Division Two: winners 1977/78
Lancashire Cup: winners 1981/82
BBC2 Floodlit Trophy: runners up 1976/77
Awards: Trumanns Man of Steel Second Division Player of the Year and Young Player of the Year – 1978.

John is at home at full back, centre,

or stand off and his deadly accuracy with the boot has secured many a Leigh victory. John gave some dazzling performances with the Lancashire and Great Britain Colts, and Leigh stepped in to sign up such local talent.

He was a member of their beaten Floodlit final team as a 20-year-old in 1976 and in 1977/78 played a major part in taking them into the First Division as champions. He scored in every game that season, only the fifth player to have performed the feat. Against Blackpool he landed 38 points - a club and Divisional record. John added the First Division record to his name in March 1982 when he scored 29 points in Leigh's 56-6 defeat of York.

His selection for the Great Britain under 24 team was inevitable and on his debut – in the 27-9 win over France at the Boulevard – John scored one try, and kicked six goals. Chosen for the full Great Britain tour of Australia in 1979, he kicked five goals in the second Test. And against France in 1981 he scored one try and kicked seven goals. John was selected for the 1984 Australian tour, but declined for business and domestic reasons.

His loyalty to Leigh was rewarded in the summer of 1984, when he was appointed the youngest coach in the club's history, following the resignation of Tommy Bishop.

Mick Worrall

Born: March 22, 1962, Warrington, Cheshire, England.
Height: 6ft 4in.　*Weight:* 15st 0lb.
Position: Second row.
Club: Oldham.

Great Britain Honours
Debut (full): January 1984 v France (in Avignon)
　(under 24): January 1983 v France (in Carpentras)
Appearances (full): one
　(under 24): three.
Club Honours
Division Two: winners 1981/82.

A strong second row forward, Mick has seen more success at international level than with his club. In 1981 he was named as substitute for the Great Britain Colts international against France. He was one of five Oldham players in the squad that day along with O'Rourke, Dobb, Seabrook and Platt. Mick progressed to the under 24's and in January 1984 made the full side for the first time in the 12-0 victory over France in the first Test. He was selected for the 1984 summer tour down under. His only honour with Oldham, meanwhile, has been the Second Division Championship in 1981/82.

Geoff Wraith

Born: October 1, 1946, Leeds, West Yorkshire, England.
Height: 5ft 10in.　*Weight:* 14st 0lb.
Position: Coach.
Club: Wakefield Trinity.
Club Honours
John Player Trophy: winners 1976/77 (Castleford); runners up 1971/72 (Wakefield Trinity)
Yorkshire Cup: winners 1977/78 (Castleford); runners up 1973/74 (Wakefield Trinity).

Geoff was one of the finest uncapped full backs of the modern era. He started his career with the Leeds amateur side, Belle Isle, before moving to Wakefield in 1963. After a long apprenticeship, he became a regular first team player in 1969. Geoff spent 18 months in Australia with Northern Suburbs in the early 1970's and joined Castleford on his return. He retired in 1983 to concentrate on coaching and was appointed by Wakefield Trinity in June 1984.

Stuart Wright

Born: March 19, 1950, Stockton Heath, Warrington, Cheshire, England.
Height: 6ft 1in.   *Weight:* 12st 12lb.
Position: Winger.
Club: Widnes.
Great Britain Honours
Debut (full): June 1977 v France (in Auckland – World Cup)
Appearances (full): seven.
Club Honours
Division One: winners 1970/71 (Wigan) 1977/78, 1983/84 (Widnes)
Challenge Cup: winners 1978/79, 1980/81, 1983/84 (all Widnes); runners up 1976/77, 1981/82 (both Widnes)
Premiership Trophy: winners 1979/ 80, 1981/82 (both Widnes); runners up 1977/78 (Widnes)
Championship Play-off: runners up 1970/71 (Wigan)
John Player Trophy: winners 1978/ 79 (Widnes); runners up: 1977/78, 1979/80, 1983/84 (all Widnes)
Lancashire Cup: winners 1971/72, 1973/74 (both Wigan) 1976/77, 1978/79, 1979/80 (all Widnes)
BBC Floodlit Trophy: winners 1978/ 79 (Widnes).

A former Soccer player on Chester's books Stuart turned to Rugby League with local amateur side Latchford Albion. He joined Wigan from Albion in October 1969 and in his first full season with the club – 1970/71 – scored 33 tries. He also won a First Division Championship medal and a Championship Play-off runners up medal following defeat by St. Helens.

His excellent wing play was rewarded with selection for the England squad for the 1975 World Championship. He scored a try on his England debut in the 27-12 beating of New Zealand at Odsal, repeating the feat on his Great Britain debut against France in the 1977 World Cup. In between those two matches Stuart moved to Widnes for an £11,000 fee. He was an instant success at Naughton Park, becoming the League's top try scorer in 1976/77 and 1977/78 with 31 and 33. The 1984 Challenge Cup success was his fifth Wembley appearance with the club and his 19th major cup final. A joiner with Wigan Council, Stuart has suffered a series of injuries in recent seasons. He dislocated his shoulder for the tenth time in March 1983 and was out for a year.

Acknowledgements
Data compiled by Ian Morrison and John Huxley, who wish to thank David Oxley and his staff at the Rugby League headquarters. Revised by Garry Pearson.